I Remembered

Recovering from Childhood Sexual Abuse

I0026170

Kristene E. Friday

Culicidae Press, LLC
922 5th Street
Ames, IA 50010
USA
www.culicidaepress.com

editor@culicidaepress.com

**Culicidae
PRESS, LLC**
culicidaepress.com

Ames | Gainesville | Lomgo | Rome

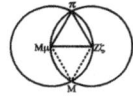

For more information, please visit www.culicidaepress.com

ISBN: 978-1-68315-009-1

Cover design and interior layout © 2017 by polytekton.com

*For Alan, my love and confidant, and for
Survivors; let your voices be heard.*

TABLE OF CONTENTS

PROLOGUE

Your memory is a monster; you forget—it doesn't. It simply files things away. It keeps things for you, or hides things from you—and summons them to your recall with a will of its own. You think you have a memory; but it has you!"

John Irving from A Prayer for Owen Meany

What we remember from childhood we remember forever—permanent ghosts, stamped, inked, imprinted, eternally seen.

Cynthia Ozick

When I picture myself as a little girl, I am running toward something. Under the hot Midwestern summer sun, I run down the blister-tarred road to play with neighborhood children; I run through the corn field behind my house to the muddy creek where I wade in and watch silvery fish dart around my ankles; I run home at near-dark, sunburnt, shins bruised, as tired as the sun collapsing into the horizon. I was always outside, immersed in the natural world, in my own little protective bubble, feeling free. Today I still picture that same little girl, long brown hair streaked blonde from the sun, but now she is running from her life, to save herself, to escape at least for a time, from the abuse she experienced and witnessed growing up in a home where she was not protected.

I thought I remembered everything from my childhood, dealt with the dysfunction of my family and left my past behind; all the ugly parts put neatly to rest. I accepted what happened and moved on but the past catches hold eventually and never releases its grip, never dies, no matter how hard and furiously one tries to bury it. A tragic piece of my past, memories long buried by my child's mind, wormed their way into my consciousness in September 2015, when at 49, I remembered the sexual abuse by my father.

I remembered.

The floodgates opened and the result was a psychotic break. Temporary psychosis. It felt as if my mind were unzipped and all of the pain and trauma of my past spilled around me. Chaos in the brain. Overwhelmed. Exhausted. Truth revealed itself and I broke open. That's what it feels like now when I think back on that confusing, chaotic time. My thoughts became jumbled; memories from the past rose like rising flood waters until I was pulled under and washed away by them. Overcome. I drowned in them.

In the weeks leading up to the break, I began prescribing special meaning to simple words and phrases as if they were a secret code I had finally deciphered and the revelations made the past make sense to me at last. A casual remark by a friend became something deeply profound; a comment by an acquaintance suddenly explained something in my life that was, in reality, wholly unrelated. It made complete sense to me then. What I did not recognize was reality was slipping away. During this time, I became focused on my past and carried around this obsessive desire to make amends for past behaviors where I felt I had wronged people. My mind would roar with thoughts and I felt an internal "Go, go, go!" and this need to talk, talk, talk, fast as if my entire body, mind and soul were being pushed by that rushing water to some unseen, unknowable destination.

It frightens me now to realize how out of control I was, as if my mind was suddenly hijacked by some unseen force, because control was paramount in my life—it's how I kept myself and my life together. It felt as if my mind betrayed me when my world crashed and I remembered the awful, bottled-up truth. Little Kristene who had been running her entire life, finally caught up to me, spun me around, pulled me down to her innocent, suntanned face, cupped her hands around my ear and whispered the secret she had held so tightly inside for all of those years.

My mind in turmoil and my world unhinged, my husband, Alan, took me to my family doctor. I was diagnosed with temporary psychosis, paranoia, and post-traumatic stress disorder. At this initial visit, I rambled on and on telling my doctor many things about my past, experiences I had never even shared with Alan, the one person I trusted the most. Some parts of that visit I recall; other parts are fuzzy or long forgotten. One memory I shared was being molested, at ten years old, by the brother of a classmate. I had never forgotten the abuse but simply stored it away, placed it high on a shelf, in the secret closet of my mind. This episode of molestation had taken place in a public swimming pool. He swam up behind me, put his hand between my legs as I clung to the side in the deep end, inserted his fingers into my vagina and said something low and degrading to me. I froze—stayed still and silent staring straight ahead until it was over and he laughed and swam off. I felt terrified and confused. I knew what he did was wrong yet also understood not to tell anyone. My doctor would later tell me at a follow up visit, she discerned by my reaction to this molestation that I had been molested before.

I was born in 1965 during a time when sexual abuse and its devastating effects were not discussed as openly as they are today. Tragically my story is not unique neither for that time period nor for this one. According to RAINN (Rape, Abuse and Incest National Network), it is estimated that 1 in 9 girls and 1 in 53 boys under the age of 18 have been sexually assaulted by an adult and 93% of perpetrators are known to the victims—80% were parents—and every 8 minutes in the United States, child protective services confirms or finds evidence of a child's sexual abuse claim. Because most incidents of sexual abuse go undisclosed or unreported, experts know the numbers are much higher. In the case of the molestation by the boy, I knew what he did was not right but who would I have trusted to tell when my own father had molested me? I reacted to the abuse just as I did when my father was molesting me—stayed still and silent until it was over.

Why did I have the psychotic break at 49 and not years before? Why did it take me this long to remember? Early in my healing journey, I asked myself this question many times and while I wanted a definitive answer I know that one doesn't exist. I finally realized it doesn't matter why I remembered and how—the importance is that I DID remember. I'm a doer, a goer, a push-through-and-get-on-with-it type, so I wanted a step-by-step guide to follow so I could heal and move on. I was angry and I wanted my life back but I would learn that healing from trauma does not work that way. It takes time. A long time. The meltdown was a lifetime in the making and there is no time table, no step-by-step chart or how-to booklet on how to heal from it.

My therapist explained I finally felt comfortable enough, safe enough, to face my past. After agonizing, initially, to understand the break and what exactly triggered it, I accepted that I don't need to understand it from a scientific point of view or an intellectual point of view. I remembered because I could only carry it all for so long. Emotionally and physically worn out, I had to stop running. My mind gave me no choice when the flood of memories rushed over me, and, like a bridge sagging under too much weight, I broke. It was a normal reaction to having grown up in abnormal circumstances. The quote "Nobody realizes that some people expend tremendous energy merely trying to be normal" comes to mind when I reflect on writing about being 'normal' and my experiences growing up. Of course, I know there is no 'normal', but I sure did try to look and act as 'normal' as possible growing up. I hid my feelings or stuffed them, all the while feeling different and alone. I did not even let Alan, my love, confidante, and supporter know my past and this was characteristic of me because in order for me to feel 'normal', I had to hide the past and the ugliness. But the mind, as I have learned, never forgets.

While I remembered, because it was time for my mind to let me, I believe the following contributed to, or pushed me along, an irreversible course to September 2015:

The previous spring, I saw the man who assaulted me in the pool all those years ago, and I pictured the molestation as vividly as if it had happened that morning. I maintained a calm demeanor while my insides broiled with anxiety and the words like, "creep," "pervert," and "child molester" flashed in my mind. I had relegated the memory of the abuse to the dust bin of my mind but here it was back in Technicolor, and there I was once more a frightened and confused little girl clinging to the side of that pool.

At my son, Sam's, college graduation party that June, my mother drank to excess and embarrassed me, Alan, and our children. The more she drank the more foul-mouthed and argumentative she became. My mother was a binge drinker who was either a happy go-lucky, 'everything is wonderful' drunk or a bitter, pitiful one hell bent from the first guzzled drink on everyone around her being as miserable as she was, and on this night she was the latter. She cursed at one of Sam's friends, embarrassing him; sat at a table with my daughter Elizabeth and her friends and asked who among them had tried pot, leading Elizabeth, mortified, to promptly stand up and leave; and made fun of Alan in front of a group of his friends. Finally, thankfully, she was so drunk she went to her car and passed out. My children had witnessed the happy drunk version of their grandmother a few times at holiday gatherings but had never seen the mean drunk version. I was mortified, furious, and disappointed because she had not behaved this way in years but I held my emotions in because history had taught me confronting her would have only made more of a scene; she would have become more foul-mouthed and angry or worse, insist she could drive. So I seethed with anger while a handful of long suppressed childhood memories of my mother's drunken behavior, accompanied by their companions of helplessness and embarrassment, surfaced: hearing her stumble through the back door yelling my name, walking down the hallway, leaning over my bed to talk nonsense to me; waking up in the mornings and finding our car parked at various wonky angles in the small front yard ashamed because all the neighbors would know she'd been out drinking again; picking me up from a friend's house hours after I'd slipped on a concrete step and hurt my lower back. My friend's parents finally tracked her to the right bar in town.

Here we go again, I thought, along with dashed hopes that, at age 71, my mother was past this behavior.

At the party I acted as if her actions didn't bother me because that's what I did. That was my modus operandi when it came to the alcoholism/the problem drinkers in my family. I ignored. Kept them at arm's length. Put up with it. Swallowed the anger, embarrassment, and shame. Except this attitude was no longer working for me because my children, Alan, and our friends were witness to the behavior. The next day I apologized to Alan, Elizabeth, and Sam and told them it would never happen again. Yet, rather than confronting my mother, I stuffed my feelings.

Elizabeth had been dealing with serious health issues all summer. Eleven years earlier, at 14, she was diagnosed with a connective tissue disorder and she had two major back surgeries to correct scoliosis—one to fuse her spine and the other to install bolts and rods to keep her upper spine from continuing to twist—and it took her a year to fully recover. It was hellish to see my daughter suffer so. That spring of 2015 she was diagnosed with an autonomic nervous system disorder after she began having intense pain in her back and hips along with redness and swelling in her right leg and foot. Then the daily migraines started. Through the years, I carried a tremendous amount of guilt about her spine surgery—always chiding myself internally asking the what if questions. What if I had not listened to the chiropractor who advised against surgery? What if she'd had the surgery sooner, would it have made a difference? What if? What if? Maybe her scoliosis would not have been as extreme; maybe she would have suffered less? A mother's lament playing like an endless loop in my mind. I read that trauma to the spine could be a cause of autonomic nervous system disorders so the guilt feelings returned in force. Accompanying her to all of her doctor visits that summer, painful, guilt-racked memories reappeared as I helplessly watched her suffer once again. By default, I blamed myself for this fresh round of health problems. And the stress and worry in my distorted mind continued to build.

By the beginning of that September, I had completed CASA (Court Appointed Special Advocate) training and had my first home visit with my child. A CASA is a volunteer who works alongside a Guardian ad litem for children who are placed in the foster care system. At my first visit, seeing my CASA child's home life was, possibly, the final trigger. We were cautioned in one session that the training and subsequent visits could bring up past memories of abuse. My emotional state was already fragile and learning about and seeing my little guy who reminded me so much of my children Elizabeth and Sam at that age—blonde, smart, and tender—brought childhood memories of turmoil to the surface. Seeing this young, innocent child living in a chaotic situation due to his parent's neglect, further inched the floodgates open.

What I remember during the psychosis:

Turning medicine bottles upside down when I had taken my mood stabilizer and anti-anxiety medication so I would remember I had taken them. Forgetting anyway. Insomnia; walking and pacing; wringing my hands. Doing laundry at odd hours of the night. Paying bills at midnight and forgetting to put a check in the envelope or record it in the checkbook. This intense feeling to hang onto reality, to routine, to strive to do the ordinary, consumed me. I was plagued by an inability to focus, forgetfulness, intense dread, panic, and fear.

Alan, driving, asking if I wanted to go to the stress center. I said no. Then yes. Standing at the receptionist desk. In some rambling fashion telling a woman I needed help. Sitting down and filling out paperwork. A small room with a table. A different woman asking for my insurance card. Asking if I was homicidal or suicidal. No and no. More questions from her. Staring at the top of the table as I answered. Same woman telling Alan to take me to my family doctor. Feeling throughout as if I were floating in a dreamy, fog-like state. Numb.

Sitting in the waiting room at my doctor's office. My name is called. Walking down the hall to an exam room. Thinking, why am I not wearing my glasses? Worrying what the nurse would think of this because she had gone to school with Alan and me. Sitting on the exam table? Or a chair? My doctor asking questions and then showing me a small chart, and I felt confused. Why is she showing me a chart? It made no sense, so I told her, "No, I have to tell a story." And then talking and talking, an endless stream of words about my childhood and teenage years. Seeing Alan sitting in a chair in the room across from me staring at me intently. My doctor turning to him "Did you know any of this?" Alan shaking his head and saying "No." More questions from her about my family; more words tumbling out and then, click, I remembered. I knew why all of this was happening but could not say it out loud. Confusion about why she didn't just turn to me and say it. SAY THE WORDS, I shouted in my head, WHY ARE YOU TALKING TO ALAN? JUST SAY TO ME YOU WERE MOLESTED BY YOUR DAD. I felt a scream building; a pressure I couldn't control but wanted so badly to manage. Control truth. Control reality. Alan talking to her, prescription written, more words between them, then walking out the door. Driving. Parking at the drive up window of our pharmacy. Alan asking me if I knew how long we were at the doctor's office. No, I said. Two hours, he said. I felt confused about losing that chunk of time. Why did I not know we were there that long? Staring down at my lap and telling Alan what I remembered but could not say out loud at the doctor's office: my father molested me.

Walking up to the receptionist's window at a behavioral health clinic and checking in. Showing my insurance card. Staring into the camera lens; angry, the woman told me to look at her so she could take my picture. Sitting on a couch, Alan at my side, across from a therapist and answering questions. Her asking: "Kristene, do you know what reality is?"

In the days and weeks following the psychotic break, in the early days of the struggle to heal, I was either thinking about the abuse or working hard not to think about it, and doing day to day tasks were difficult; the anxiety and depression always present, ready to overwhelm. What saved me, besides the support of Alan and therapy, were my journal and pens. They were by my side throughout the weeks and months following the psychotic break, when it felt as if the ground would open up and swallow me. I had to journal about my experience for my past to make sense, for me to make meaning of all the pain, anxiety, fear, and confusion I was feeling. If I could not write about what was happening, it felt as if I was going to lose myself forever. Throughout the brutal process of facing the truth, grieving and healing, writing kept me grounded, helped me hold on to reality, to feel as if I would survive what felt un-survivable. In essence, writing saved my bacon.

The temporary psychotic break and PTSD kicked me in the butt both mentally and physically. Once an educator, with two university degrees, I struggled to find words at times or I would forget how to spell a word which, before the psychosis, would have come easily to mind. I struggled with memory loss, panic attacks, fatigue, paranoia, and extreme anxiety. For weeks, my mind was so jumbled I could not drive somewhere unless it was short trips to known destinations near my home.

How I saw myself as a woman, how I saw the past, how I dealt with relationships, changed seemingly overnight. I felt different. The same but not-same me.

What follows are verbatim excerpts from the journal I began two weeks after my psychotic break. While I wanted to use my real name, for legal reasons, my name and the names of those involved, have been changed. It chronicles the first year of my healing and grieving process from September 2015 when I remembered to September 2016.

I use the initial B when referring to my therapist and Dr. G when referencing my doctor. At times, to provide clarification, I include additional information in parentheses.

SEPTEMBER

11:15 p.m. 9/22/15 ??

can't sleep

Worried

Pacing

Anger sadness fear all overwhelm me.

I hate not being able to sleep—I've always been a napper. Used to love napping with Elizabeth and Sam when they were babies. I stress over not being able to sleep which only compounds the symptoms of PTSD. I just want my life back or a "new life" or what I thought my life was with the three most important people in the world to me: Alan, Elizabeth, and Sam.

Scared how quickly my life changed—wish I would have had the psychotic break earlier in my life—then how my life would have been better? Better partner to Alan, better mother to E and S—"I followed the handbook" I was so glad to hear Elizabeth say that. So glad Sam is telling me "Love you, too" when I tell him "Love you."

Hate this. Can't concentrate long enough right now to read a chapter in a book.

Keeping paranoia in check—getting meds under control—will take time.

All the repetition behaviors that suddenly appeared didn't really suddenly appear—gradual over time??

Mistakes, regrets, everyone has them—they just swallow me whole at times. Immobile, frozen, disgusted with myself.

Pride in my children, lucky to have Alan who is understanding and helpful. I'm ready to be more independent again. Medicine working—getting sleepy.

On the couch—want to sleep with light on—TV is on and I can sleep it's just reminding myself that I CAN—that is frustrating.

"Normal" or "Abnormal"

All families are dysfunctional there is no "normal"—thank you B. Therapy/letting go/giving in hard to do.

Façade/"I've been living a lie" thinking now of an animated movie I saw with Elizabeth and Sam—with a dog in it saying this?

Meditate. Let go. I've come far—Alan—touch helps. I just want to talk, talk, talk and get it all out and be done with it. NOT how it works. Slow my brain down. It's not that late but I am so tired. Tired of trying to hold it together—snapped. Thank God. A great relief in a way.

Writing helps. I know this.

9/25 1:45 a.m.

Will be a while sleeping through the night. Swarming bees dream during a nap. I am tired. Body aches. Just want to drive and think—best time to remember. Paranoia. No normal family. Dysfunction is normal. Meltdown. Memory work hurts. Mistakes learn from them. Follow the handbook for child raising. I had to. Compliments hard to hear at times. Write or my soul dies. Fight for myself—let go of everything else but what I need to heal for myself. Doing what's necessary. Tired at 22. Tired now. I want to stop being tired. Escape. Go. Go. Go. Rest. Sleep. Would I have taken my own life? Thought about it—long ago memory of disassociation; of feeling split in two. But would not have done that to the kids…would not do that to them.

9/25/15 3:16 a.m.

At least waking up later and not doing strange things—paying bills and making mistakes, nervous walking/pacing, and other things I can't recall. Coping mechanisms—working on them. PTSD read online extreme form of anxiety—long period of time to recover—longer if do not receive help—longer it takes to heal. My father molested me. Truth. Lies. Family.

Dreamed of bees swarming—had not had such vivid dream that I recall this past month when meltdown started. Meltdown. Kinder word than psychotic break says B and that's fine with me. I need kindness right now. So waking up later in the night is good. Yes. Good.

Still problem remembering all said in therapy sessions. Still chunks of past recent and further back missing maybe never to return. Worried about cost of therapy. Maybe should go one time a week? I go two times and it's helping, that's all that matters.

Happened before I was ? Before ? 5? If it happened later than 5 or 6 say ages 7, 8, 9, 10 or 11 when parents separated and he moved out wouldn't I have remembered it? What is blocking it—not ready to remember specifics yet—maybe my brain would explode. NO. No shame no blame. My new mantra.

Remembering house on Jones Road one night crying in bed listening to parents fighting. Wanting to go to Leah's room for comfort. Wanting to run out and yell at them to stop but I couldn't felt frozen.

I was good at faking what happened to me growing up. Pretend my life was not what it was. People had it worse. Lash out, laugh, cry inside, hurt, anger—let it out/don't confront—trying to figure it out. Take my meds—vitamins as B said to call them —I always felt different—always have but I'm still me—almost. Meltdown happened when it needed to ?—just can't go back to where I was—and that is good. Grow, change, strengthen. It's part—this meltdown—is part of my story now. I am still me. You're only as sick as your secrets.

Practice being?....? not me but I am me that's ok. I'm open, kind-hearted compassionate—I'll get myself back.

9/27

In the quiet I can hear my thoughts now—disorganized rapid fire has calmed—meds working. Memory better? PTSD Post Traumatic Stress Disorder. Extreme form of anxiety/depressive disorder—write or lose my mind. Writing is therapeutic I knew this; I journaled a long time ago and it helped. I said those words—where did I go? Self-esteem—I had it once—I will get it back.

Depression seeing myself/split self. Knowing what I was doing but just went on. Muddled through. This is what I did in the past. Ignore the text; the noise. Stream of consciousness writing I'd tell my students. Now it's me who has to write this way or I will go mad right now maybe forever but I'm back. I'm trying to get back. I'd like to SCREAM. Why? Just let it out.

So many friends and family who love me yet I feel alone today not always but today right this second. Stop doing what you've been doing Kristene—I can't run from this. I can't make it go away. I just want to move on from the past—will be pulled back I know it but I will be okay. I'm a different person now. Amy (*a friend since early childhood*) told me I'm doing brave, hard work—so does Alan so do the people I trust. My life melted down…my mind broke. I'm relieved. God bless you B. God bless you medication.

Taking care of who I trust and love and most of all taking care of me. Working at letting go of my worries…well almost. Breathe deep. Take deep breaths.

OCTOBER

Oct. 1 4 a.m.

I hear the words Aren't you done being sad yet? No no not yet. Some days weeks, months, never? Yes I will be done with sadness someday I hope. Life changer. I know now why my mind broke. Why? My life was screwed up enough was that the root cause? The molestation? Domino effect that, then this, then that. Trauma is trauma. Age event. (*B asked me to hand write my earliest traumatic memories relating to my family of origin—my mom, my father, sister and myself. I listed my age, the event and in one or two words how I felt at the time. It was grueling work and I was going to therapy twice a week; simply going to therapy was physically and mentally exhausting at this time because I was forced to think and talk about painful memories I had never shared with anyone, not even Alan*). Feeling…ugh. One more page to get through then one more thought to think about the past. 2 steps forward 1 step back or 1 step forward 2 steps back. It's about me. My healing what is necessary. I can't do it all anymore. Let go let God. Al-Anon wisdom I need again. God tapping me on the shoulder: Hey, it's all about you now it has to be or I will go over the edge. Tipping point thought upon thought. Move, go, move forward I'm ready, long overdue.

Memories. Inability to show anger—TELL ME! Just say it. Another failure on my part—NO. NO. NO. Life. They are who they are. Let it happen. Stop controlling "whatever" smile. Mountaintop beauty, dogs in dresses, love again. Switchbacks mountaintops extreme curves fog friendship renewed. Redemption. But wait—keep at arm's length. Withdraw. Step out. In the light. Don't look at the negative. Darkness. Stay in the light. Listen to the story. No patience today. Tomorrow yes. Next day maybe next day and so on and on and on.

This is a grief. Coping skills. New normal. New life. Hang on. Surround myself with supportive people let go of relationships that no longer work for me. Falseness. Eh. No time at all for that. Love, kindness let me give it. Receive it. Let me let people help me. Stop covering. Stop going along to get along to keep the peace. Keep MY peace, not theirs. You give more than you get—someone told me that once long ago. I thought yes yes you were right then and right now. I'm too tired to behave that way anymore. Age, wisdom, turn the page Bob Seger, new chapter, renewal. Hurt. Hurt again. Love, hurt, madness, sanity. My brain cracked open and broke; lifted up and healing.

Oct. 1 afternoon
Good—better for me now. Session not as draining this time. Feeling sad but not completely wiped out. Sad. Sad. Sad. Positive thoughts, no shame no blame. My new reality.

Repetition over and over and over. Helped to talk. Just talk. Going to stop minimizing, apologizing, prefacing. I will be me—I can be me. Processing it all afterwards is draining but B said two more sessions and then this part (*the age/event exercise*) is over. Long road but I want concrete follow the directions steps—the manual to be KRISTENE again. She's there and coming out—spontaneous carefree loving compassionate outspoken a human being who needs to be herself.

Sun. Oct. 4 9:10 a.m.

I am going to stop reading about childhood molestation and memories—when I do my heart starts pounding and I feel anxious. I am having trouble concentrating enough to read and I love reading. My brain/body won't quit churning. Today I didn't wake up until 5 a.m.— my normal wake time when I was teaching. It was fun being with Elizabeth yesterday and finding a house with her—it's perfect for her. (*Elizabeth had bought her first home an hour north of us where she works as a school counselor.*) When she talked about school things it made me miss teaching but I know I can't do it— physically or mentally right now. Or ever. I'm too tired for much except doing work around the house and bookkeeping (*for our farm*). I will make an effort to get out of the house—I do and I will continue to do because I have to but it wears me out. I feel like I have to be "on." When will that feeling go away? I know everyone puts on some kind of mask for the world. Mine just feels really heavy right now. I have two therapy sessions this week and then I'll be done with my past inventory of memories—my age/event paper. It leaves me shaken. Feel okay; pause for therapy session; crash; feel okay. Then once a week therapy. I'm just SAD.

10/4 3:15 p.m.

Worked in the yard and that helped anxiety. Dead-headed daisies and sprayed weeds. I planned on going to CVS (*a pharmacy*) but the thought of running into anyone I knew caused a panic attack. I'm already worrying about Tues. session—I took my list *(age/event exercise)* out of my purse because just having it in there made me anxious. I'm going to be okay. My memory is getting better. I'm looking forward to a new year. This past month. This meltdown month and the memories of my childhood. I'm ready to heal and live life healthy in mind, body and spirit. I'm sleepy now. Silence. Relaxed. Want to write write write. I'm listening to my body and I want to be myself but a better, truer version—one day at a time. Al-Anon. (*I attended Al-Anon, a support group for families and friends of problem drinkers, in the mid-2000s when my sister relapsed and was arrested for drunk driving and stealing prescription drugs. My mother, as always, came to me to "fix" things and bail Leah out of jail, which I did twice. Once again I was pulled into the insanity of my family and I did not want any part of it. I was, as I had always been, embarrassed and ashamed by Leah's drug and alcohol problem. I had no understanding of addiction then and enabling behaviors. When I received a third call to bail Leah out of jail, I refused. Someone recommended Al-Anon and it was a godsend because in the meetings I learned about the family dynamics of alcoholism and how to detach and take care of myself.*) I thought about going to a meeting again but not ready yet. Cannot sit around table and listen to stories of women and men living with their alcoholics. Angry at the alcoholics in my family right now. I know I survived this long because I am strong.

Therapy is writing and writing is therapy. Want stacks and stacks of blank journals. Dad. Fuck you. There are not enough pages in the world for me to write those words when I think of you. Of what you did to me and Leah.

I just wish I could focus to read. That is bothering me. I am just used to keeping it together and it's rough so rough not to be able to do this. I need to remember to tell B about my panic attack—that is important to remember. I will remember because my memory is better. I laugh, I laugh, I always laughed. I don't want Alan, Elizabeth or Sam to look at me like I'm crazy or treat me any differently. I am still ME. I just need to cry and cry and cry at times. Stay busy. Keep moving. Depression. A black blanket thrown over me. Heavy and wet.

The month of September
Missing pieces fragments
Broke brain
Broken pieces now
Fragments of who I was then
Shards fall whole again
Writing will preserve my sanity
FEAR
Forget
Early memories not all
Armor myself
Reality new

I need to touch Alan and my children. I need that contact the hugs, the I love yous I need the person I was to them. I can't be that same person anymore and I'm scared.

Mon. Oct 5 7:47

I realized I like writing down date, day and time—gives me reassurance—helps with tracking days. I feel like this will help me get my mind back on track. I go from tears to dealing to panic attack mode to full on panic attack when thinking of my past; my family. I am taking ½ tab of Klonopin in the day so I am not zonked out—it is helping with anxiety—duh Kristene the meds are helping. I want to sleep the past, the dealing with the past, away but I refuse to do that. To be like my mom in that way. I am sad about the "sad" parts of my life as anyone who has gone through what I have would be. The line 'quit being a victim' runs through my head but hell, Kristene, you were a victim. Embrace it—that child who saw and went through crap and came out ok—ALIVE. I remember now the first time I had suicidal thoughts. I was a sophomore—16— this was when I stopped eating and then it turned into binging and purging on and off but can't recall how long that lasted? It ended by my senior year, before then, I think. B said to tell her if I remember this because it could be important.

Control. Yes my life was out of my control and I hated it. HATED the things going on at home then. I would be fine, would deal, or feel happy and then another hit would take me down. I would deal and then something I was angry or fearful about would hit me like a wave and drag me under. I now realize that's been happening my whole life.

Happy then some event = fear, anger, sad/depressed, depressed—sad, angry. Depression on & off on & off.

Oct. 6 4 p.m.

Finally through the age/event/emotion exercise with B. (*After this session, when I finished talking about traumatic events from my childhood, B told me to tear up the pages when I was home. I couldn't wait that long. Standing outside of a Norton's Deli where Alan and I stopped to eat lunch, I tore the papers over and over again and then watched the tiny white bits fall into a trash can. Relief. A purging. I talked about the trauma, I tore the papers, and the memories held less power over me than they had my entire life. Until then, I did not realize the weight of what I was carrying.*) So glad—it was rough but cleansing/freeing— remembering and talking about these things leaves me tired physically and emotionally. It ended with the man who stalked me and almost came into the house to attack, rape, kill, abduct me—God knows what. During the session, I didn't want to talk about it so I folded my paper and put it in my purse but B said, "Anything else?" I had talked through everything but this so I pulled the paper out of my purse and told them about him. Afterwards B said, "Talk about anxiety!"

I was in the 7th grade. The first time I noticed him I was with Julie at an ice cream place on the square—the Sugar Spoon. He had a military crew cut and he stared at me, his hard, black eyes bore into me as he walked by and I made a crack about his haircut something like Buzz, Buzzzzz, Buzzzzzz and we laughed. Later on a school day, he parked in our neighbor's driveway after following my bus home. I was on the phone in our family room talking to Julie—wearing my bra and underwear or bra and shorts, a pink bra with small triangle cups that snapped in the front. I was talking away and I briefly turned toward our French doors and his face was in one frame of the glass. Glaring, ugly, menacing cold eyes, dead eyes. Just staring at me but his presence didn't register in my mind. I kept talking and then I looked at the door in our kitchen that went to our garage and the brass handle was slowly turning back and forth. I don't know if it was locked or if I ran and locked it. I do know I screamed and kept screaming and I ran back to the phone telling Julie what was happening. She asked if she wanted her mom to call the police and I told her no—in my child's mind I thought I would get in trouble for making fun of his hair as if that was why he was trying to get to me, as if the entire situation was my fault. I felt guilty, the one to blame for his being there. Finally, the fear overwhelmed me and I told her yes to call the police because the handle was still slowly turning. I hung up and ran to my bedroom, locked the door, put on a shirt, and begged and begged to my bedroom walls and ceiling that he was not walking down the hallway to my bedroom. I recall peeking out the bedroom window finally and seeing the back of his head in a blue car driving down the road. My emotions swirled. Frantic. Blue car, four door, dark military buzz cut, he followed my bus, waiting for our neighbor to leave for work. How long had he followed, stalked me? Mom pulling into the driveway, me running out to her screaming, sobbing. The sheriff showing up. Asked me questions. Mom said we'll get a big dog, went home after school to a neighbor's house for a few weeks. Felt awkward. Mom told me they caught him but later when I was older in my 20s? 30s? we were talking about it. She tells me she lied to me. They never did catch him. He didn't go to jail like she said he did. Why not let me live with the lie? I was so terrified to be alone for a long, long time after that happened. I remember the rumors at school: I was raped, I made it up, it never happened. So I stayed silent. I shudder to think what could have happened. The mom in me shakes her head. Why I didn't receive counseling after this? Why didn't we talk about it? It happened. Get over it. Move on. That was the message. That was always the message.

We sold the Jones Road house because Mom couldn't afford to make the house payments anymore after the divorce and I do recall ?? she wanted to move because of bad memories and the man who stalked me was one of those memories among many.

Deadbeat dad. Dead dad. If my father weren't dead I'd want him dead. He was one sick bastard to molest us. I KNOW I KNOW what happened to me. It is important that I remember all of it. I want the young child Kristene to remember everything.

Oct. 7 6 a.m.

Yesterday evening I threw out pictures of my father. I had two pictures upstairs—both from when he was in high school—threw frames and all in the trash. Went to basement—mom has boxes of things stored from when she moved years ago. Went through pics and threw out every one that my dad was in and the few that evil creep boyfriend of mom's was in as well. Put them all in a trash bag and took them to the dumpster where they belong. Visualized them smashed into the trash truck and mixed with all the garbage WHERE THEY BELONG.

Reality is what is real. What happened. My dad molested me; he molested my sister. Ages? How often? These questions I may never have all the answers to but I want to know it all. Ultimately is just knowing it happened enough? Yes and no. If he were alive I would confront him.

I have to have compassion for myself right now and for the little girl inside me. I can only take care of myself. I do not have the energy to worry about anyone else. I feel FREE for the first time in my life.

I felt guilty all of my life because my dad verbally and physically abused Leah. I remember that. Mom did nothing to stop him. Enabler. Echoes of verbal abuse; that's what I hear. I was never beaten by him. I was the compliant child. I was his Little Shaver, his "favorite" or so I was led to believe, but that didn't stop him from molesting me. Sick, sick man. But I survived—I have a wonderful life. I've traveled, have a great husband, two beautiful, intelligent, caring, well-adjusted children who are successful. I've made mistakes. Everyone makes mistakes and has regrets. No shame, no blame.

Fear. Anger. Guilt (shame)—be aware of when and why I feel these emotions. Anger is my best friend right now. I'm fearful of booking a flight or hesitant to see Amy (*a lifelong friend*) in November. Why? I don't know. It's not like me. Am I afraid I'll have a panic attack? Plane will crash—no. The uncontrollable—yes. Today I am going to seriously look at flights and choose the least expensive one and message Amy about fly in/out days. I REALLY need to see her. She's always been there for me no matter what.

I used to obsess about sleeping. I just wanted to sleep—depression, forgetting the world. Tired. Tired of life sometimes. I don't want to feel that way anymore. I want to live a full, wonderful life; one that I am unafraid to walk through. I want to be brave. I am brave. I want to trust. I will trust more. I will trust my intuition—that still, small voice inside me. That adventurous, curious Kristene who was independent and smart and creative. I will look to her and trust her and what she wants and needs not selfishly, forgetting others, but to take care of her—for once just her. I will work every day to do this.

Healthy coping skills—that is my goal—that is how I will not lose my mind—not meltdown again. I've melted down I am now on the other side of it. I take my "vitamins" and I'm better for it. I'm starting to cry from relief—relief that I survived. I didn't kill myself when I thought about it during those dark times in the past. I had to live for Elizabeth and Sam and Alan. I couldn't do that to them. Depression. Mental illness. My body and mind holding onto the ugliness—the molestation, the violence I witnessed growing up, the times I buried what I didn't want to feel and say. The pain. It overwhelms.

Oct. 8 5:25 p.m.

I wrote my letter to Dad and sobbed throughout. Had to take a break because it made me feel sick.

I liked today's session because the psychosis has passed and it was the real me talking to B. Relieved to be back. Relieved when B confirmed the psychosis was over. Felt out of my mind but relief, relief, relief to know why I have struggled on and off all these years. Called Leah (*my sister*) and left the message B said to leave. I said my part and now I will let it go until B tells me otherwise. She is my guide through this and I can trust her but I know if she says something I don't feel is right for me I can refuse to do it. I need to pull back from negative people, situations, movies, TV shows etc anything that causes me to feel more anxious. I bought a small journal to keep in my purse so when I feel overwhelmed away from home I can write.

Oct. 9 3 a.m.

Leah agreed to meet me for lunch next Thursday praying she doesn't cancel so I can have any information that will help me. Even better if she agrees to go to a therapy session with me.

B asked when I think molestation started. Was it before I was 5? From birth to when parents divorced? Where did I go when I left my body while it happened? Counting. When I get anxious I would count obsessively sometimes in twos, sometimes in single digits. I've done it all of my life—still catch myself doing it now. Is that what I did? Looked away. Went into a trance; a fog.

I am glad I feel more like my old self. Memory is much better—do not feel need to excessively talk about it. Waking up startled at night has lessened too.

No longer scared of what I will find out about my past. My body tells me that. I am now in charge of my body and feelings. I'm letting go of the fantasy that my dad was a good guy and any compassion I had for him is gone.

Help me God to remember the details—through dreams, music, anything. I can handle it. Must handle it to heal. The past will not defeat me. I can live with this. Praying Leah tells me her story to help her and to help me heal.

It comes in waves I can have a good morning or a good stretch then a song, any irritation will set me off then it's crying and thoughts that I don't even know why I'm crying. It's my heart. I do know why I cry. Just let me be sad, just let me cry. What's wrong? What's wrong is that I discovered at 49 that my dad is a child molester. It's going to be okay. I know, I know, I know, I know. Psychosis is over. I'm worried about Alan, Elizabeth, Sam what this is doing to them. I'm worried about…fill in the blanks after blanks after blanks. I can't see B next week and that is okay. I refuse to slip back into old habits. I won't let the past win.

I spend my mornings crying and writing. I am going to walk upstairs, shower, and watch TV. Right now everything is magnified 200 times. Who am I? The poem assignment. If I weren't tired and feeling calmer I'd write one. I'm safe now at home no one can hurt me.

Oct. 10

Positives: Elizabeth buying a house. Sam farming full time with Alan. Life is good right now.

Worries: Elizabeth's health, what Leah will tell me BUT I will be able to hear it. I will listen and be patient.

I can't write the words "I hate you Dad" enough. Not enough reams of paper and ink on this planet.

Oct. 11

Feeling calm today. It is frightening to me to realize how scared everyone was, which now that I'm outside looking in, it even scares me. Psychosis. Psychotic break—those are scary words. I can understand why B told me to call it a meltdown and my meds vitamins. I was in a terrible place but now....relief at this moment. Didn't have to take anxiety med today until we were going into town to eat dinner—my mind was fine with it but my body was saying Whoa! Danger ahead. My father. Memories. Had this idea, which was a terrible one, of driving by the Jones Rd house but couldn't do it. Why I thought I needed to, I don't know. Like it was some kind of test or something of my resolve.

B said to notice things that make me feel panicky or uneasy—specific songs, places, situations. Right now being around people who I've tolerated in the past but who really bother me or I dislike increases my anxiety a hundred fold soooooooo Kristene you need to be more REAL and do what you are comfortable with.

What if I had not had the meltdown? Would I have turned into what? A crazy person? I melted down before so many ugly things could happen—divorce, suicide, my children hating me, me hating me. Alan and I not growing closer as we have. Now it's time to be okay with the pain and the reality of my past.

Gratitude list today: valuing my health both mental and physical

Alan, Elizabeth and Sam

Our beautiful home

The fall weather

Friends good, true friends

Speaking of friends, going through this has made me realize who is worth my time that's for sure. I'm grateful for that knowledge.

I need to let go of outcomes trust God and let him do the work so right now this very moment that's what I'm doing.

No shame no blame. Hoping and praying Leah feels comfortable enough to open up to me and tell me something anything that will help me; help me trigger my memory; understand that time period of my life. God, help heal her and lead her to get help. I pray that she will come to a session with me. But boundaries God help me to continue to maintain boundaries so that I stay healthy. As B said, never give up. Never give up.

The cycle of abuse, of domestic violence. I broke the cycle. B told me this and I cried. I was so so tired and I lost myself, but I'm me again—different but better, stronger even though I feel weak.

I can't believe this is my life now. Is it my life? What is my life? It is me in this bed right now writing. It is Alan asleep beside me. It is Sam downstairs on the couch. I am so scared God. So scared. Scared of the dark tonight. Did my dad make me scared of the dark? Yes. I was sleepwalking before I turned 5. Night terrors from age 5 to 10. Sucked my finger until the divorce when I was 11. Depression on and off, on and off. ANXIETY. I'm afraid of falling asleep. It's going to be easier to sleep with the light on. I've gone as far and as fast as I can. I can't run anymore. Severe anxiety x 100. I thought I didn't need my anxiety med today but I was wrong. Panic feeling;

fear. I need to write instead of talk like an insane person—everything churning, spinning in my mind. PTSD. Molested by my father. I feel like I'm going to lose my fucking mind right now. Sleep. Please sleep.

Oct. 12 7:36 a.m.

Ended up sleeping some last night. Nights are hard since the meltdown without my anxiety med. Memories need to come out or I will explode. I don't dream or if I do they are gone in the morning. But today is going to be a good day. Going for a pedicure; run errands and to meet Elizabeth around two o'clock when her home inspection takes place. I pray all goes well with it—the house is 20 years old and roof needs replaced and they are doing that so there should be no major problems. She's happy about the move and we are happy for her. Exciting time of life for her. God has so many good things in store for her.

Sam went to see friends last night. I'm happy the guys had a day off from harvesting. They needed it.

As for me, I will make it through this. Reality is what happened; not what I think happened; the fantasy family I wanted to remember; the pretending/denying I did. The forgetting. I need to accept it. My heart is pounding right now just thinking of this truth.

Oct. 13

Elizabeth is having MRI of her head for migraines she's had since end of May. I'm keeping it together. I'm working at living in the present moment right now. B said to always live in the present and it's hard but I'm working at it. Kay (*a friend*) and I are having lunch tomorrow she's picking me up at 11. Looking forward to it and grateful for her friendship and support.

The sound of the MRI machine is loud, industrial, annoying and making me nervous but it's doing its work. It's a 30 to 45 minute scan so Elizabeth picked out a movie to watch to keep her focused on something other than the scan and the claustrophobic feeling. God please let the results be normal or if there is something let it be a simple fix. She's my baby girl please let her be okay. Surround her in your protective light. I'm keeping it together for her, for me, for everyone or so it feels that way.

At session today told B of a night terror from my childhood. I was in my parent's bedroom lying next to mom and I was screaming and she was holding me. I remember feeling like I was trapped by something and was awake but couldn't fully wake up. Dad was pacing the bedroom. Was I in my bed when the night terror started or was I sleeping in their bed? I always wanted to sleep with them because of bad dreams. I can see the bedroom, the heavy red curtains; gold four-poster bed, mom trying to calm me down but I couldn't stop screaming. B. said my dad was pacing because he was nervous that he would be found out. I know this truth now. I'm learning to look at my childhood before the divorce in a new light. The lens of reality. The reality; not MY distorted reality. What my mind has finally let me see.

Leah may or may not tell me her story on Thursday but I will be okay with that. If we had received the help we needed, had we been protected, had truths been faced, our lives would have been healthier. We survived despite the abuse. That is something to be proud of—both of us. We are doing the best we can; we did do the best we could. I can forgive many things. I can have immense compassion for people. What my dad did is a crime and unforgiveable. I'm angry as hell as I should be. I need to be angry right now. I need to feel my real feelings. Real. Do not turn it inward. Do not minimize what happened.

Walked down for the mail this evening—guys are working at Briarwood. Depressed but not feeling disconnected but there's still the what if? What if I filled my pockets with dead-weight stones and walked into the water. I can now clearly and intellectually understand why someone would. It's overwhelming and the idea of not having to feel this way and having an out is tempting. In the past it was a hazy depressed state and the thought of taking my life was a brief flit like a hummingbird flying around my head. Darting in then away. I will not do it and I don't want to do it but I used to think people cowards who would take their own lives but they are not cowards. They are people in pain who made a choice in an emotional state that was overwhelming and clouded by mental illness, depression, despair. I turn my thoughts away from darkness to what I have now and ahead of me. I'm an intelligent, funny, caring woman with an amazing future in store. I have Alan who loves me as much as I love him. I have wonderful, kind, funny Sam and caring, sweet, funny, tough as nails, Elizabeth. They are both so tender-hearted and this is the best quality Alan and I could ask for from our children. They care about others. They care about themselves. Self-care. Love yourself. I hope Alan and I have left them, imprinted enough, the qualities and capacities for love of self and others.

Thursday 10/15

Met with Leah. She wouldn't tell me specific information—too hard for her to talk about. Said dad did molest her many times. Physical, verbal, emotional abuse too as I knew. Leah said the physical abuse happened more often than I remember—I blocked so much. Hard to hear. She cried and said she can barely keep it together for herself. Did not want to talk about it; said she had moved past it and didn't want to think about it. She hasn't moved past it. I know that. She did ask if she could go to a session with me. Of course, I told her that's what I want for the both of us to heal from this. She's wrong about moving past it. You never move past it. You survive it and find a way to live with it.

Friday Oct. 16

My worry book. Writing calms me. Tired of repetition when will that stop? Is it part of the process or medication? My memory is still lacking. What helps curb my anxiety: writing, staying at home, walking on treadmill, going places with safe people—friends I can trust. I fear if I let it overwhelm me I will never leave the house and I don't want that to happen— agoraphobia. This is not like me. I loved to go places, and now that I second guess myself constantly it feels unnatural to me. Who am I? I want to ask Dr. G if repeated thoughts/ repetition is part of psychosis or side effect of medication. Honesty. Since taking Brintellix I have started having thoughts of suicide. Suicidal ideation. Not feeling that I'm going to do it but thoughts are still there. This new symptom appeared last week. I'll tell Dr. G about it. I felt really good and now sadness, I know this is normal but before Brintellix suicidal thoughts were not there. Did not pop into my mind and then disappear. Felt too "normal" to feel them and that's the scary, perplexing thought.

Dr. G visit went well. She said the forgetfulness will go away in time. Stopping the Brintellix. I had taken medication from a similar class in the past she said and had the same side effect with those as well. Said Brintellix was a bridge to help get me through the psychosis.

Alan and I are going to dinner tonight. Normal.

Oct. 16 4:30 a.m.

Mood lighter—no persistent thoughts of suicide. Not sleeping only exacerbates my anxiety and depression. Trying hard not to think of the past—live in the moment - and this week I'm doing a better job of that. Looking forward to a few days in Michigan with Elizabeth—a terrific diversion.

Bought my first piece of Roseville pottery—beautiful green vase with pinecone in center. Found it in a shop in Chesterton. Looking forward to more finds in the future. Maybe will find a piece in Michigan?

Oct. 18 3:18 a.m.

Here I am up at 3:18 in morning. I had a thought that this psychotic break, this meltdown, has made me into a new, better?, person. More real. Real me. I feel different like I've "come out." I can be me—angry, sad, feel my real feelings without hiding, running. It's time to focus on myself now. I've taken care, sometimes cared too much in unhealthy ways for people and did what they wanted or I did things to please them and I wasn't being true to myself, to my wants and needs. Meltdown liquid now a solid—solid Kristene. Since September, because of September, I'm finding out, realizing, acknowledging my past, the truth, what I knew inside but stuffed the feelings, smashed the truth down. Right now I feel disgust when I think of dad and what a pathetic, sick person, parent, to touch your daughters, to molest, harm them. I'm no longer freaked out about knowing this. It happened and it was what it was—extremely sick and disturbing. All families have some dysfunction, as B said, but mine was extremely sick and dysfunctional. I wanted my family, the four of us, to be as "normal" and healthy as possible. I did survive and succeed under difficult circumstances. I was resilient and I'm okay and will continue to be okay. Life is good. I have two beautiful, amazing children and I protected them from my past as long as I could. And then there's Alan, my protector, love, and friend. My imperfections I embrace now instead of hide. I want to live, love and laugh and enjoy my life. And I will.

Oct. 19
Today is going to be a good day. Sun is shining. Elizabeth and I leave for Saugatuck tomorrow. Taking dogs to kennel in a little bit. Then what? I will work in the

basement organizing and getting things together to take to Goodwill. I have to keep busy—that is what I need today. I may read later or not. Patty (*a friend*) texted to see how I was doing and I replied truthfully. I began crying afterwards, teary on and off since. The past hurts—bringing it to light hurts but it's a necessary hurt. I'm still telling myself it is okay to cry at the drop of a hat over anything right now. How much effort it took, the toll it took on my mind and body to repress, suppress try to forget my past. The HURT. Read somewhere ? when a person has a terrible childhood it often doesn't come out until around my age. Read on a PTSD blog I joined this has happened to others into their 50s and beyond when they remembered molestations. That made me feel not so alone. Thank God I have the life I have. Working on giving myself credit for what I've accomplished against difficult circumstances.

Accept my past and God help me do this and move on each day. Over and over. One day at a time. I'm going to work at not letting the next "hit" in my life drag me down, depress me. Whatever comes, I am working to know that I will be okay. Look what I've overcome already. I have to be here for myself and my family—be the best, healthiest I can be. I see B Thursday at 3:30. When negative, dark thoughts appear I am going through my mental gratitude list. I need positive diversions and Kay and Patty (*friends*) have been checking on me. God truly blesses me with that. Let go of the past. Let go of the past. I work at telling myself it is okay to be sad—I have a right to be sad. My meds keep me above the waterline—no drowning, Kristene. Allow yourself to be sad and taken care of today.

Oct. 22 early a.m.

Saugatuck trip was quick but enjoyed time with Elizabeth. Found a set of Roseville bookends in an antique store, very interesting pieces and I had not seen them before other than online so I bought them. Elizabeth found a couple of pieces for her new house—a white table she's going to use as a nightstand and an old window she's going to make into a coffee table.

The diversion of going out of town, that feeling to just GO, is one that I cannot escape. No escaping the inescapable. I drove up there and back because I had to be behind the wheel, had to have something to do other than ride and think. Control. Let go, let God. Thank God for the Al-Anon phrases… nuggets of wisdom that I've stored in my head. He wasn't the dad I thought I knew—before the divorce and even after. I'm tired of feeling down. I am working at feeling empowered by the meltdown—to see it as an opportunity; it has changed how I feel about myself as a woman and how I feel about my life—past, present and future. Right now that is courageous, optimistic, and exciting. Turning 50 in 30 days and looking forward to it and the future living life, for the first time free from the past; unencumbered. I finally slept so well last night. Did not wake up until 4:30 and that is a breakthrough for me. Wonderful sleep.

I see B at 3:30 today and have 3 appt's lined up for the next 3 weeks. It's a comfort knowing that I have appt's made in advance. Plan on finishing an embroidery piece today and look into taking a crocheting class. Need to keep my mind and hands busy. Plan on taking more things to Goodwill—

donating things I no longer want or need makes me feel good. Cleaning. Organizing. Trying to make order. In my mind and in my life.

I'm working at, will be honest about what I need and want and communicate that with no apologies, for the first time in a long time maybe my entire life. Breathe deep and let go and sleep peacefully. Sleep because God holds me in the palm of his hands. Trust all will be ok. I can't control others but I can choose how I respond, live and live healthy free from the alcoholism in my family. I have always been ashamed of dad for abandoning us, discarding us like we were meaningless trash. I am okay with feeling this way. I am okay with saying and accepting that I grew up in a home with alcoholism, verbal, emotional, and physical violence. Pretending takes too much energy. I survived all of it. I'm working on loving myself and increasing my self-esteem. I feel less exhausted now after experiencing a flashback or trigger. Live in the present. The past is behind me and I am working on leaving it behind me—releasing the pain from my past that I've carried with me.

2:29 p.m.

Early for my appt with B. Nervous, too. What will come out in therapy today? I'm holding it together. Came by myself for the first time. It felt weird driving this route myself. Glad that I can finally drive further from home with confidence and without getting lost. Knowing that I'm going to talk about the past makes me nervous—feeling sick to my stomach. Sitting in the parking lot thinking about my past and how much I went through and that when my mind broke from reality—how it all poured out during and after. Now I have to face it and it's a struggle. I hate my parents for their alcoholism and their choices that scarred me and Leah. I hate dad for what he did to us. Anger at them keeps me from going under when it all is so overwhelming. Remember I'm in the beginning, the very beginning of recovery patience, patience, patience.

Oct. 24 3:46 a.m.

Trying to figure out, adjust my meds so I sleep better. It's a process, frustrating, because insomnia is adding to my anxiety and depression. Memory/forgetfulness still an issue and that's frustrating me, too. B said at therapy this past week that 80 to 90 percent of women who have fibromyalgia, studies have found, they have been sexually abused—Wow—shocking to hear but understand why. Holding in the pain causes emotional and physical hurt. I am making myself do things, getting out, it's easy for me to stay home where I feel safest. I want to get past this feeling and B says it's going to be at a pace that works for me. I have been go, go, go and it's exhausting. Part of me wants to stay busy to not deal with my feelings, to not take time or have quiet moments to just relax, remember and FEEL my feelings. I'm figuring out my life; this new normal and it will take time to do that. Remember struggle leads to growth. Trust that I am moving in a positive direction. Thinking about the past when the wet, heavy blanket of depression covered me. I don't want to go back to that place. Those were long, hard days of struggle. The disassociation, the sheer weight of trying to be normal, acting as if nothing was wrong. In a trance, unable to ask for help. I made it through and my prayer is that I never,

ever go down to that dark place again. I'm feeling very tired but I believe, I trust, I will be whole again.

Oct. 25 6:35 a.m.

Slept very well until 2:30 and then read for a while. B recommended a book *The Body Keeps The Score*. Started it last night—fascinating read—how the mind/body are connected. Recognized myself and my actions and behaviors because of my traumatic past. Began crying so put it down. Lines I relate to:

"repetition leads only to further pain and self-hatred"

"strong emotions can block pain."

"the greatest sources of our suffering are the lies we tell ourselves."

Interesting how the mind works. Lies covered up my past but I avoided the truth and pretended when I was young that my life was something it wasn't. Just wanted, desired, to be someone else. I was me but not me—not true to myself. I longed for a life, a future that was different or better. I wanted out of my circumstances.

My goal is to not overthink, over analyze, stop worrying and waiting for the other shoe to drop. I'm tired of being sad and tired.

Oct. 26 Monday 3:15 a.m

Woke up had feeling, saw image, felt sensation of Dad grabbing my crotch—anger coming from him. He was helping me get dressed, or trying to dress me. I was 3 or 4 or 5?? Little. It was early morning, light was new, coming from a window to the left of me. I felt warm and disoriented. Tired. He was angry because I wasn't cooperating and he grabbed my crotch. No words. Just grabbed me in anger like a parent would grab a child by the arm to make them stop doing something and held on. Felt like I was standing beside myself watching it happen as if I was there as both child and adult. Need to tell B this.

7:20 a.m.

Went to church yesterday it was comforting and I let the tears run down my cheeks and did not try to hide I was crying. Felt good to be there felt present and prayerful surrounded by love, trust, and acceptance. I can't sleep but sleepy and I'm learning that's ok. Insomnia sucks but it isn't going to last forever.

I am relieved I had that flashback—it just happened. My body is letting me remember and it feels good. Very good. I am open to receive all the memories of the abuse. I trust that I will be okay with whatever flashbacks I have. Trust my feelings, my knowing and my remembrances.

Oct. 27 2:18 p.m.

At session with B. talked over my flashback—seeing him grab my crotch in anger. Validation of what I knew had happened and my mind had buried. B said she wants me to keep journaling.

Told B after last session, I was exhausted and had a bad, very down day. Felt achy all over, especially in shoulders.

Oct. 28—I remembered the date without looking at my phone. 2:30 a.m.

What I remember from Sept. these are the thoughts running through my mind. Alan taking me to B and at first visit my thoughts were scattered, all over the place, hard to focus, to make sense. Patty coming to visit me. Alan telling me she was coming to the house. I had typed out something for her to read because I couldn't say what had happened, asking her if she believed me, needing to hear that she did, her saying yes, I believe you. Later, telling me she cried the whole way home. Two pages of age/event/feelings timeline B assigned. Hard to go through the past and talk about it all. Alan taking me to therapy twice a week until I could go by myself these last 2? Or 3? Still having time/memory problem. Told B yesterday about feeling as if having social anxiety—certain places or situations make me nervous. Things that used to not bother me or maybe I was a little nervous about REALLY make me nervous— magnified, loom large in my mind. Going to see Amy already worried about it—flying, what are we going to do, what do I talk to her about. I used to not be like this.

Feel like a child again at times insecure/scared/confused. I want my confidence back or I want to be in a place of security.

Thinking of the past and my first memories both positive and negative.

Happy had a big litter of puppies, all black, lived on Northwest Street. Lying on grass, sunshine, warm letting puppies crawl all over me, puppy breath, licking my face, laughing.

Waking up in a closet, standing against a wall, confused, wearing a long nightgown, my dad or my mom feeling *(one of)* them touch me, talk to me softly, leading me back to bed.

My mom crawling, drunk, parents out drinking dad asking her, trying to get her to bed, he seemed nervous, by the front door. Had he taken babysitter home already? I was 4 maybe 5. Leah would have been 9 or 10. How embarrassed she must have been. I felt confused and sad.

Sleepy now. Going to stop writing and try to sleep. Thinking about the past wears me out. PTSD result of what happened to me. My body is remembering. Positive messages, I'm OKAY. My dad was a sick man. I am understanding that now. I do not forgive him yet. I want to and B said I will get there. I can't forgive yet.

I'm working at being aware of how I feel—working to stay in the moment. Remembering is tiring.

Oct. 28 2:10 p.m.

Had a massage—the body does keep the score for sure. Saw the image of Dad helping me get dressed, holding onto my shoulders, see his frustration, helped me into my underwear and clothes, his anger—so intense, palpable. Since that flashback my upper body has ached esp. my shoulders as if my dad's grip in anger were still there, the anger still inside them. Felt good to have the tension released—feel like it's gone—feel lighter now, happier. I had a few moments of fear during the massage, the awareness of being alone in the room with the massage therapist even though I go to him regularly, I felt aware of my breasts pressed against bed, nervous, had I not taken Klonopin this a.m. I probably would have felt the claustrophobia overtake me. My claustrophobia has worsened over the years. I trust my massage therapist but the question entered my mind—what if he touched me? Grabbed me? I worried briefly and it passed and massage felt GREAT.

Oct. 28 5 p.m.

Rented the movie Southpaw but became agitated and angry at the scene where Jake Gyllenhal is squatting in front of his daughter and talking to her when she is in foster care, whispering to her, telling her he will be back for her. This was a massive trigger—had a panic attack and began sobbing, picking at my nails, agitated. I was fine until that scene—his daughter didn't want to see him. A memory surfaced of Dad whispering, telling me something, a secret between us.

Breathing deep, I feel angry, sick to my stomach. Southpaw was a poor choice today. Scary feeling passed through me—terror, anger so intense that I've never felt so deeply before like my chest was going to explode. Feel hot and sick.

5:20 feeling forgetful again, wanting to open my day planner and look at it, for what I don't know. Somehow it anchors me, keeps me sane at times, the days of the week in small boxes next to each other. Each day if I have something, something to do I will be okay. Staying in present moment, positive thoughts, no worrying, you can do this. You can get through this.

10/29 4:12 a.m.

Woke up thinking...my mind trying to make sense of my life now—words in my mind trying to achieve writing about my past thinking about it—it's there the words making sense in my head but putting on paper is hard. Can't write about it.

Worn out from last two days—from insomnia from thinking too much from triggers. Crying comes too easily but I know I have to, my body has to let it out. Happiest thinking about plans to go to FLA in March for a couple of weeks. Happiest thinking about Alan, Elizabeth and Sam. Thinking of my CASA kid thinking of anything but ME my feelings but as B said I finally feel safe to let it out. The it. The abuse, molestation, witnessing verbal, emotional abuse, physical abuse. Guilt that Leah bore larger brunt of our dad's sickness. Or did she? I just don't remember all of it. Tired of keeping it all inside. I can't hide from it anymore. I want to. I don't want to think about it. Who Am I? I am a Survivor. Writing this makes me cry because I'm sad about what was done to me what I saw, what I hid from but happy that I am here—I did not end my life, turn to drugs or alcohol—I'm still here.

I turn 50 soon and I realize now that I'm in this place right now and it happened because ???? my mind just went blank. I know but struggle to put into words, make, put puzzle pieces together of how I am here, how my mind melted, broke and how I am different now—honestly, the truth is exhausting but liberating yes that word makes me smile and sigh in relief. I don't have to hide anymore, run, I can stand still now. Stop and know and feel. Going through this has made me let go of so many petty things I used to care about. The being myself but not myself letting it out, no holding it all in, cost my mind and body. I've made progress. I've accepted this, this new normal. How has this changed my family? In ways I don't know. We're closer yet I feel set apart from them, a stranger to myself and them at times and that is frightening to me and more tears come now thinking of this. I'm grateful I can now cry so easily. I have no time now for the trivial in life. What I hold onto desperately is my family, the people I trust the most, very few but at least I have that, B, medication, the mundane comfort of the everyday—doing laundry, cleaning the house, shopping for groceries, necessities, keeping my life orderly and normal, comforting, routines my lifeline.

Alan—no secrets between us now, he knows my past, all of it now, finally as B said after going through the age/event/feelings "homework" we've grown up together now. Perfectly imperfect. Perfect is what I wanted to show the world—hide what happened to me. In my head I can hear echoes of my past, those words that make me feel small, need to hide, stop writing down the truth. Don't tell, live a different life, create something different, done. Don't show your real self, don't speak the truth because what if? Denial, repression, suppression. Focus on my healing, of seeing it all for what it was. If I don't, I fear it will cost me my sanity.

I keep going when all I can manage is leaving the house to run errands, to be in the world for a brief moment, learning to accept that this is what I can do for now. Practicing gratitude, acceptance, forgiveness the thought of forgiveness is there but I don't feel it yet. I have a clearer picture of who Leah is but she doesn't want to talk about the abuse with me and that's her choice. I choose a different path—to live to work at living the truth of why I am the way I am, how I lived, to give my children a better, different life than I had.

I read about good parenting, followed my instincts, over protective. I tried. I made mistakes but time to let those go.

I am not alone in this. I just could not face it until now. I'll be okay. Alan the kids and B. won't let me drown. Trust issues. I need to accept that I'll always have them.

Oct. 30 11:49 a.m.

Going to try taking only 5 mg of Risperdal—the full dose makes me feel numb, flat. I'm nervous about leaving the house—just going to run errands but it's making me nervous thinking about it. I want my life back! Stay in the present. Positive thoughts. I am a beautiful child of God and I will get through this and come out stronger than before. I recall a fragment from September. B smiling at me and saying "You broke the cycle of abuse" "You were the white sheep of the family" feelings of guilt about it then and sadness as if I have survivor's guilt. All of this has to mean something. I have to feel there is a reason I am going through this; something bigger than myself.

3:29 p.m.

Alan called to check in and it helped talking to him. Working out my meds is frustrating trying to find what works best. Feel like I'm going to crawl out of my skin. My anxiety is making me pace, wring my hands and forget things, or makes my mind feel muddled. Writing furiously helps me focus, centers, grounds me.

Picked up a prescription for Belsomra—sleeping pill— only bought 10 very expensive at $10 a pill. Worth a try if I can sleep. I want energy to live life to the fullest now. I've spent too much energy not being me—hiding me and there's no time for that now.

Just messaged Sam—he has been so loving and caring of me through this. Thank you God for him and for Elizabeth. The joy they have brought me—no words for it. I worry that my depression and anxiety affected them growing up. Guilt. I am really going to have to work hard at letting go of GUILT. Tears and more tears. Where does this extreme guilt feeling come from? I have so much anger, guilt and fear. My mind held onto so much for so long, too long. I felt safe enough to let the truth out but it felt like I couldn't, it wasn't possible, to not hold it in, to not meltdown. Timing—the kids are adults now. Alan is my teammate. Safe. Mindfulness. Thinking about my thinking. It was time to begin healing from the past.

Oct. 31 7:01 a.m.

Didn't have to look at my phone to check on date so I take this as progress. I'm remembering. Last night slept okay for the first time. Woke up at 1 a.m. when dogs were barking in the woods. Thought again about the Northwest Street house and my happiest first memory with our dog Happy and her pups. Clean, crisp image. A good memory.

Saw a picture yesterday in paper of a child molester who had been arrested—felt rage and anger. I've stopped watching the news—cannot handle any negativity of any kind. I'm trying to keep it together and I can easily become anxious, sad and distressed right now. It's like my insides have been flipped open, exposed, raw.

Thinking about Mom and I am angry about her choices and actions when we were growing up but know that she had an alcoholic father who was violent and abusive. It's the cycle—no surprise there—that's how it can go. That's how it went in my family. Transgenerational B called it.

Take care of myself focus on getting and staying healthy, love my family and friends. Think about and make choices I'm comfortable with…when there's so much noise in my head and panic fills me, stop and breathe.

NOVEMBER

11/1 4:30 a.m.

Thinking about writing and how I recall from a writing workshop I went to long ago one of the speakers said a person must write his or her truth before he or she can really say what he or she needs to say. Realize all the sadness I poured out in some of my fiction writing was the sad, lonely girl inside speaking. Depression was there for a reason. The ties that bind. The ties that choke the life out of you. I refused to lose that spark of light, life in me. I stayed strong for that little girl in me. I stayed strong for Elizabeth and Sam. Be a different, better parent that voice said. I was. Not perfect but better. I was always here for them even when I was at my lowest. Always protected them. Thinking about my past, those fragments, the shameful, embarrassing parts, the anger, how I was so tired and how it took so much energy to live. I thought that was normal.

My tendency to focus, stray into other people's lives to avoid thinking about my past has to stop. I'm improving focusing on my well-being—mind, body and spirit. Overall, my focus is better. Thank God I can focus to read again. Figuring out, making sense of the world, my world, the inner me.

My past has cost me enough. Gratitude, gratitude for what I have today. I've lived a charmed life. Wisdom. Age. Tough times many, but many good times too with Alan, Elizabeth, Sam and my friends. I see the image of a scale—one side is the dark, negatives in my life, the other the positives. Picturing the scale the good events, good memories outweighing the bad. Rising above. Visualizing it.

Stop letting IT dominate my thoughts. IT = my past, my parents, my sister.

Shame, denial, guilt, fear, anger, caring too much at my own expense.

What was real?

Real: alcoholism, drug addiction, domestic violence, molestation, sexual assault, eating disorder, hatred of self and others, embarrassment, abandonment, pretending happy, loneliness, fear, sadness.

Confusion, I'm different, lies, truths, reality of my father—he's dead, several years now thank God, easier to cope with all of this because he's gone. "Dead to me long ago" said this when talking to a friend about my dad's death about a year after he had died. I was sad when he died, cried, hell spoke at his funeral, feel like a fool now but I didn't have the knowledge, the knowing, the remembrance of what he had done then or I wouldn't have gone to the funeral—how did Leah stand being there?

Silence. Survival. Moved on but I didn't really. Faith— it carried me through. Willpower.

Truth, courage, happiness, honesty, love, authenticity. Words that have more meaning—deeper shades of depth now.

Nov. 1 5 p.m.

Be a truth-teller. Keep my courage—don't let go hold onto it. Breathing, staying in the present, writing my story to keep going. Look at the past but without anger—when will I be able to do that? Went to church, walked dogs, worked in the yard, therapeutic. Tuning out the world so I can face the world. Working at staying in tune with my wants, listening to my body and mind, silence, without judging myself.

My dad molested me. How far I've come in two months that I can write those four words without hesitation, without it making me feel sick, without it making me want to burst into flames from the anger. Thinking of the one memory I can recall of him beating Leah. Dragging her from the dinner table, such sickness. Where did all the other memories of his hurting her go? Will Leah ever share them with me? Will she come to a session with me? I don't know; I hope so but I have to let that desire go—no control, no energy anymore for the illusion of control.

Nov. 2 4:50 p.m.

Woke up out of sorts but plowed through—kept moving. Drove up to Elizabeth's house to drop off some things, ran errands, had lunch with Mom. I had anxiety about it—first time I've seen her since the meltdown. Working on not avoiding people who trigger my symptoms. Had an enjoyable time with her—she didn't bring up the past as she is prone to do. Tired of that a long time ago. We just talked and it was normal mother/daughter time.

Only time sadness creeped in was when I was driving back from Elizabeth's house—tears came and I let them. Do not fall into a pity trap Kristene. I don't feel sorry for myself I feel ??? confusion, deep sadness about this whole situation, about the meltdown about not being able to prevent, control it. Working at not withdrawing from the world because it's easy for me to do, too easy. I try not to be needy but right now I need hugs, understanding, tolerance, love, patience, independence and this feeling I have of being dependent is alien to me. Scary. B said to share everything, all of my thoughts and feelings, with Alan and I try to. It's just foreign for me to do that. He's been supportive and this has been rough on both of us—do not forget that Kristene.

Fantastic news: Elizabeth's MRI came back and showed no abnormalities. Thank God. We may never know what is causing the migraines, her neurologist said, because so many things can trigger them. I just pray they simply disappear one day.

Nov. 3 8:30 a.m.

Woke up angry. Just angry. What did I dream? Can't recall but the dreams left me feeling out of sorts.

Kay, Sarah (*friends*) and I are going antiquing and then to lunch. Beautiful day, sun shining. An outing. Love these. Important to keep going, doing. Any new place I can see makes me happy and makes me feel alive.

Still experiencing extreme anxiety, nervousness around people in social settings with friends. Where is this coming from? Trying to pinpoint it. Lunch and shopping was fun but I was ready to come home. Ready to go, ready to come home. I never felt anxious in social situations before and this is irritating to me. Routines are important to me—routine-oriented, rule follower. I don't like feeling out of control—when I was a teenager and I would screw up, it would shake me to my core. Depression. I'd make a mistake and it would send me into a tailspin. I could have fun, let go, but only to a certain point and if I messed up I would feel so guilty that I would become depressed. When I told B this she said it's a sign of childhood sexual abuse. Theme in my life: sailing along, take a hit, and boom, I'm down.

I'm working on seeing things as they really are. Not running away from issues I don't want to face—people, feelings.

Accepting that there is no cure for PTSD just management. Don't like this—want it gone. I can say the words out loud or in my head but it's hard to feel that this is okay. I want to be fixed. Ridiculous I know but it's controllable. This is my new normal. Working on breaking old habits—obsessing about being "normal" is one of them. STOP. There is no "normal."

Working on not letting the past swallow me. I have to be okay each day with the sadness and crying. I'm not as exhausted as I was a month ago, therapy doesn't leave me as tired and drained.

I finished the book *The Body Keeps The Score*. It helped me understand why I feel like I do—the silence, the isolation of trauma, how it is hard to put into words what happened to me. It talked about the fear, rage, collapse that comes from trauma, that these are natural outcomes of being traumatized. It is okay for me to simply exist, to BE for a while just as I am with the feelings I have—all of them.

On our way home from lunch, we spotted a large white cross along a roadside near (*the town of*) Bean Hill and stopped. Two benches sat in front of the cross and a box with little pieces of paper and pens inside, nails and a hammer. All over the cross, were prayers on white papers fluttering in the breeze. I wrote down a prayer for Elizabeth and Sam—to have faith, hope and courage in their lives; and the prayer that I make it through this and stay healthy in mind and body. To live truthfully, to give what I can and accept my limitations. It felt empowering to pound the prayers into the wood.

Nov. 4 5:20 a.m.

Going to ask B today about drug-free insomnia option—maybe hypnosis? What is real to me today—thinking about, worrying about my fears. Accepting past. Worried last night about my memory loss. Cycle of forgetfulness and tears, crying feels good it's just instinct not to cry—the numbing, the avoidance.

Going through this, walking through this inferno, has made me realize who I can truly trust, to be my real self with, honest self. I question when doubt comes to mind about trusting people. Alan said he sees improvement in me and in my heart I know I've come a long way from September. Trusting it, this feeling of changing, of improving, my head is the problem—that doubt that creeps in; the fear. Today I looked at the beginning entry of my journal on 9/22 and I want to write down all that I remember about my meltdown, the things, the connections I believe were related to what made me snap but right now that is difficult—to sort it out—maybe I will be able to do it later. I'm feeling more energetic, more clear, but still feel stuck at times. Stop. Start. Move on—I will be able to. Positive energy. Difficult to give myself any credit yet I am proud of myself, can say that now, of all that I endured and I'm okay. Thinking of Max (*my father-in-law*) and how before his health declined he was so complimentary of me—always supportive and positive—of my parenting and that meant so much to me; still does. Thinking of Alan and how long we have been together—through all the good and bad—we are stronger now as a couple. I believe that. I know that is real.

Affirmation for today:

I am a strong, loving, smart woman. I can give of myself and trust others knowing that I have boundaries and I will not feel guilty about maintaining those boundaries. I can express my feelings knowing that even if others disagree with me I will be okay. It is not my job to make others happy. Relationships are about give and take. I respect myself enough to know that my decisions that are in my best interest are not selfish interests. I want to, no I am going to, live authentically and accept myself and others as they are.

Difficulty: opening up to let others see me for who I am.

At session with B today she said the anger I felt at that scene in Southpaw was a flashback. The tears, the explosive anger—an anger that I'd never felt before was a flashback. Felt reassured after she explained this because that intense anger from deep inside was frightening at first and overwhelming.

Can finally acknowledge while all families have some element of dysfunction, mine was extremely dysfunctional. It was a relief hearing her say it and I cried. Told her I hate being considered a victim or being thought of as a victim and she said that little Kristene was a victim but that today, the adult Kristene, is not. More relief at these words.

B said to buy something the child Kristene would want and my first thought was a soft blanket because of my memory of Dad coaxing me into throwing my favorite blanket into the fireplace. Telling me I was too old for it. I loved that blanket—my security. An important part of my childhood. So I'm going to look for a fuzzy, cozy blanket I want. A way to reclaim something special and important that was taken from me by him.

Nov. 6

At airport waiting to board flight. Tired and relaxed ready to get out of town ready to not think about this struggle. I am going to stay in the present, read, laugh, enjoy seeing a new city and enjoy Amy's company. Relaxed because I'm escaping for the weekend. Alan and I talked about going away for a weekend soon. He needs it with everything he's been through with me and now his mom. Her going to assisted living is a major life change—hard to leave your home, most likely for good, after 50+ years of living there. Acceptance. Change. Life.

Flying over the Rockies thinking about "floating rocks." Smile at this remembrance of camping with a friend's family when I was about 12 and as we canoed how the water rushing past the rocks made them look as if they were floating. What I thought I saw, what I wanted to see was not reality. This image made me think of how my sense of reality and the past when our parents were married, of who I thought Dad was, was not the reality that we lived. Leah saw the water rushing past, I saw floating rocks—what I wanted to see, what I was told not to tell at such an early age. She had a different perspective. I was too young to know that what was happening to me was not right…how to say no, to tell…trusted adults who could not be trusted. I know that the memories I've buried are coming out and will all be made knowable; this is scary but I know I can handle it, will handle it.

Nov. 7

Ready to visit Amy but now homesick—Kristene make up your damn mind. Wanting to be in two places at once. She scheduled a massage for me as a bday present—so sweet and thoughtful. I left my day planner at home and I wish I'd brought it—want to look at it now—look forward to what's next. My mind wants to be done with today—go go go—but have to live in the present be present. Be okay with where I am right this second. Realized it's been ages since I've flown anywhere by myself. In a way, this was a big step—I pushed through the fear I had of flying out here by myself and being just Kristene with a good friend. Not Kristene who is…Who am I? Right now I'm a woman trying to come to terms with her past.

Amy shared a memory of when we were in middle school and I asked her to come with me to the Holiday Inn to see my dad. Why the Holiday Inn? She said we swam. She said I told her I didn't want to go by myself. It gave me shivers hearing it. I didn't remember this but it's no wonder I wanted her to go with me, I had a deep feeling of fear of him. I always felt uneasy around him and now it makes sense why. I recall a time when he picked me up, I was in middle school, it was just me, Leah never went, and we ate at a hotel bar near the airport?? I recall feeling uneasy about being in a bar yet happy to spend time with him. Dual emotions—conflicted feelings about him my entire life. After the divorce, he became a stranger to us. I always wished he was a different dad. I believed his lies for a long time. Now I see the image of him taking money out of grandpa's wallet when he had taken me to see him and grandma at a friend's house—there was a dock and we fished. I was standing in a doorway and he grabbed money out of grandpa's wallet and said, "Let's go." We left like thieves and I hated feeling like an accomplice to it. Somewhere there is a picture of me holding a fish I had caught that day. Dad was a liar, molester and thief who stole from his father, stole his daughters' childhoods.

Monday Nov. 9

At Denver airport waiting to board flight. Mixed feelings about going home—ready to be home but sadness, anger, agitation all mixed together because it means facing reality—the stress of life even the small tasks that used to not be difficult or stressful are looming large in my mind: bookkeeping for the farm, therapy, Elizabeth's doctor's appt for her headaches, worries. Overwhelming feelings. None of this was hard to handle before the meltdown. Worn out. Good, much needed trip and Amy listened and was supportive. It's the re-entry into my life that is going to be hard. Kristene there is no permanent escape. Sadness is just settled inside me— just there. Depression is there and it won't be forever—it will ease. I will be better. I tell myself this over and over. Positive thoughts—look at all the good in my life. Gratitude. I smile. Happiness, I felt it once and I will again.

Nov. 10 Tuesday
Had bfast with Patty and Camille (*friends*) for my 50th birthday. Did not feel like celebrating, tired from the trip, but went with it, made it through.

Moving on—I do not like what I had to go through to get here, to be me, but it's my past—not proud of it but yet in a strange way I am—proud that I turned out okay. I'm not feeling ashamed anymore of what happened.

I felt a change in myself, a shift, as I flew home— looking out at mountains as I flew out of Denver—beautiful, rugged, unique—flying through clouds, turbulence, bumps along the way—looking at those mountains, the terrain, made me not afraid anymore. I realized how significant my life is, how what I went through as child and teenager and young adult made me, shaped me into this wonderful, chaotic, loving, unloving person. Perfectly imperfect. I am here for a purpose. I can feel the meaning of my life—the experiences—I always wanted to believe there is a reason for this suffering and at that moment flying over the mountains I felt that purpose. Not wife, mother, daughter, friend but just Kristene—the little girl and the adult—coming together and feeling, knowing, saying to each other we're fine, we're going to be okay with each other.

Dreams have returned since the meltdown and I take this as a good sign that my mind is mending, that I'm finally sleeping a restful sleep even if it's only for a few hours. I've stopped being obsessively worried about Elizabeth and Sam and how they are handling seeing me go through this—Alan talks me through my worries, talks to them, reassures us all. They will be okay—I KNOW and BELIEVE this now.

Even when my depression takes me to a dark place now, I think how I've been to even darker places—the thoughts of suicide in the past—the scale could have tipped but the kids, my deep love for them, saved me. The little girl inside saved me, the adult me was a mess. What price was paid? I look at the past because I have to, I can't help it now, but I am also looking forward more and more, and the past recedes for a time. I'm healing. B said: Little Kristene was a victim adult Kristene is not. Let the tears come. You've earned them.

Nov. 11 4 a.m.

Yesterday was rough, the exhaustion, had strange dreams, felt teary and "sad sad" as Alan said last night. I was just and I am some days just "sad sad." So here I am at 4 a.m. eating grapes, drinking a Diet Coke and writing. My memory loss still there at times. Felt proud of myself for visiting Amy on my own. It has been years since I've flown anywhere alone. I think back to the bravery I had, the fearlessness when I was younger, I want that bravery back. Elizabeth and Sam brought out a new bravery in me. Mom bravery. Protective. I hope, know, trust that I will feel whole again. I still struggle to find words that I want at times. Old words, old thoughts of hiding, not showing the real me, hiding how I feel inside try to hold me back but I can't go back. I have to move forward to un-stick myself. Writing helps me stay above the water line. Today is a busy one and that is a relief. I'm meeting Elizabeth at the neurologist—it's a comfort for me and for her to be there with her through this. Then I have therapy at 12:30. I still feel anxious about going but at this moment I'm okay—no fear of my feelings and what may come up in therapy. Crying last night and having Alan hold me helped me through my deep sadness—he's my free therapy. Love. After therapy giving Leah a ride home from a car dealership—her car is getting worked on—ambivalent about my relationship with her, how broken we are, what our past has cost us. No more words about this now. Then dinner with friends.

This week I plan on Christmas shopping and working on re-packing things in storage in our basement—family dishes, pictures, knickknacks mom saved when she moved. Grateful that I have time to write about what I'm going through—I have that time and it's a privilege. Writing = healing. My meltdown, the break, has made me a different person but as I'm sure I've written over and over I can at this moment say I'm better for it. I have a love/hate relationship with it.

"You are only as sick as your secrets." When I feel the urge to give into the despair what am I afraid of? Give into it—float with it—imagine it carrying me along until I come to a riverbank and I can stand up and walk onto the shore. The water, the feelings, won't drown me. I can make that choice.

I have choices—I am choosing to let go of old ways, old habits, of thinking, a rebirth—this process has made me stronger. I may not feel strong right now but I'm finally feeling and facing my past. I will continue to grow, to be stronger.

Nov. 11
Notes from therapy session:
Say "concerned" instead of "worried"
"faith instead of fear"
Silence—need this to refill my bucket.

Nov. 12 5:56 a.m.
Woke up feeling clear-headed for the first time since all of this began—another shift has occurred. Profound sadness has lifted and I feel really good right at this moment. Cried yesterday at therapy and cried the day before—sadness/heavy blanket of despair lifted. Cleansing—let the crying out, let it come, don't fight it as is my habit.

Working at only positive thinking, positive inner dialogue. Feeling happiness—not that internal fight going on in my body—that has lifted too.

Have massage today—excellent therapy to release the tension in my body. My arms and legs—all of me feels weighed down, this persistent physical ache. Holding in all of my past—releasing depression, old hurts, pains, shame, fears.

It's going to be a good day. I'm bday shopping for Sam, Christmas shopping and running errands.

No longer feel guilty for the good things I have in my life. I earned them. I deserve them. I deserve happiness. I carry faith with me every day and I can feel a lightness outweighing the dark finally.

Working through the past, facing reality and moving forward that's my choice and it's a healthy one.

Nov. 13 Friday the 13th 6:44 a.m.

Feeling relaxed—good day yesterday—did not have to take a Klonopin and that's a major improvement. Mind and body tension lessened—feel like I've made it over a hurdle or threshold. I try visualizing my brain healing and my body. It helps…meds, therapy, mindfulness all helping, coming together now. Still working on not feeling ashamed at times by what happened to me, shame, too, of psychotic break, feel like I should have been strong enough to not let that happen. Acceptance of that. Not a weakness, an awakening. This healing is like doing the Cha-cha—one step forward then a few steps back. Finding peace with what happened to me that's the goal, complete and total peace. Easier for me to forgive Mom—she didn't leave us. She worked three jobs for long time to support us, keep a roof over our heads and that was not easy—recall the struggles, what we went without, but also mindful of what we did have and grateful for that. There was always love from her. Grateful I am not an alcoholic or drug addict. I have a mental illness but I am managing it. I used shopping, food, other people to avoid the pain and now that has ended. I am truly healing from my past.

If Dad were alive today, if I could confront him what would I say? I would yell at him, say how could you? I see this happening, the anger, rage inside released. I would cry and scream and feel the hate and loathing and confusion all at once. I was confused and scared and sad when he hurt me so many years and this hard work of feeling and facing the pain, moving beyond the hurt, will take time. Writing, thinking, letting go— I'm ready for the next, better phase of my life. Who am I? I am a survivor of sexual abuse, domestic violence and the family disease of alcoholism. I'm crying and I let the tears run down my cheeks but I am also smiling at the relief, the sheer relief that I can even write these words, that I no longer have to be silent.

Each day is another opportunity to learn, grow, heal and let go. Be present.

Elizabeth closes on her house. Proud of her for buying a home on her own at 25. Sam is going to work on equipment in the barn and enjoy the day working on his own. As for me, I am going to relax and sit back and not worry about anyone else or myself. Faith instead of fear. Love instead of anger. Acceptance. Turning 50 soon and happy to begin a new decade of my life both mentally and physically healthier—REAL—the real me who accepts the past and lives in the present.

Sunday, Nov. 15 5:10 a.m.

Going to a party today for a classmate who is turning 50. Nervous about it—makes no sense to me that I am already thinking about it. It's the old me that I want back—never anxious in social settings. Alan and I talked about it last night. Told him how I feel exhausted at times; want to not think about the past and as I write this I know I'm repeating my words, my thoughts. Why is it hard to transfer the words in my head onto paper?

I feel nothing at times, an emptiness, no feelings, and that is scary, this numbness. Thinking of Dad this morning as someone else's father, this detachment is comforting.

We are having a 21st bday party for Sam and I would much rather think of that right now.

Reading *Perfect Daughters*—dog-eared many pages that I relate to—the sexual abuse, violence, alcoholism. Helps me make sense of how I came to be where I am, feel less alone in all of this. Reading this and thinking of my Al-Anon meetings. Reading about alcoholism helps me understand the disease, my family, my role in my family. I was embarrassed by my family's behavior so I covered up by trying to be perfect, to be the opposite of them. I know this and I shouldn't be but I still feel a lingering embarrassment, shame. This thinking, overthinking, at times is hard work, this recovery, and I don't want to do it at times but no choice, no choice, no choice. No way out but through.

Feeling a freedom as a result of this work—the grand Fuck It because I had the meltdown and now I am the real me, my past is laid out before me, all of it and I'm facing it. No pretenses.

Elizabeth and I bought meditative coloring books — another way for me to try to relax. Self care. I told Elizabeth how important it is that she have outlets for stress relief because as a counselor she needs this—she knows this but the mom in me has to remind her because I worry about her emotional health in this career. She's a helper and caring and sensitive and will always need to take care of herself in a helping profession.

Love. Gratitude. Trust. Have the first two, working on the last one. But remember, will always have trust issues soooooo accept that.

It's easy to hold onto anger, I'm working at letting it go. Anger is the easiest path but I don't want to be angry anymore. Why would I want to hold onto anger? What is the allure? It's the natural, immediate response but it only hurts me in the end. I have to rise above that, will rise above it. Working at stopping the negative soundtrack that plays in my mind, the guilty feelings, the I'm-undeserving feelings. I deserve good things in life, I have a terrific life and I've earned it. I HAVE EARNED IT.

Nov. 16 3:28 a.m.

Went to the party yesterday and felt anxious during it as if people would have heard about my meltdown but then thought how? That's ridiculous. "Paranoia will destroy ya." And then I think so what? Everyone has their issues. Talking, reminiscing about high school made me uncomfortable, brought up painful feelings. Made me feel awkward and hyper-alert. At least I laughed a little and talked, socialized. Felt anxious last night and slept some but just need to write so I can go back to sleep. Last night, like every night, I held onto Alan as I felt loneliness and fear bubbling up. Had to cling to him and finally let myself feel and cry. Where will all of these honest feelings and truth take me? I fear having another meltdown but then I think I'm getting the help I need now and I have support. No Fear—Elizabeth's tattoo. I picture it. Think about what she went through with her back, all of that pain, and I cry and look at her as my hero in many ways. She endured all of that pain and I feel the guilt of that and I let it go for now. I did the best I could with the tools I had.

My past. The psychotic break. I see an image of an egg cracking open and yolk spilling out.

Read in *Perfect Daughters* how sexual abuse is more common in families with alcoholism. I am not alone. Truth is an opportunity to grow now. New life. New beginning. Feel more compassion, more empathy, more honest, raw exposed but honest.

The party—I felt drained afterwards. Had to get myself mentally "up" for it but I did it. I put on my mask, my make-up, dressed well and went even though I struggled with going at all. Easier to stay home, to avoid, to isolate. Alan won't let me. I won't let myself—no dark thoughts of killing myself now—these are gone—hopefully for good. Sadness. Grief. Be okay with it. Ride these feelings out. Life is hard. Hell, I know that. I've not wanted to remember, to think about the past but it came forth, won out in the end. When I feel the urge, the panic rising, to cling to something now, to avoid feeling, I am going to stop and think about it. Slow down. Heal. I see waves, warm waves, washing over me. Hold onto that image. That feeling, the comfort of that.

Nov. 18 3:57 a.m.

Feel achy as if every nerve in my body is irritated, tingling, sore, a low-burning fire. I'm tired of being tired. Thinking about today's therapy session and what will come out of it. Nervous but not panicky and pacing at least. Feeling what ? Happy, sad, angry, confused, emotional, loving, compassionate, compassionless. Overwhelming.

No longer feel the "Let's go, let's solve this, fix yourself, Kristene" feeling. No energy for that. No desire anymore for that. My bday present to myself this year: honesty, healthy mind, body and spirit.

1:09 p.m.

In therapy session, B said I'm doing everything that I'm supposed to do to help myself. Told me I'm a good student—those words made me feel good. She said I had a flashback after the party, the stories brought up the memories, the reminiscing, thinking about high school, negative memories, things that had happened and I tried to forget. This was why I was teary Monday morning and out of sorts and drained. She pointed out that connection to me. I'm working at changing my thinking. At understanding. Wanting to recognize why I'm feeling the way I do, why my emotions are so raw, so vivid, why I feel turned inside out at times.

The three of us discussed having a family meeting with Elizabeth and Sam—giving them an update so to speak. I am ready to do that. Have the four of us sit down. I have been worried about what this has done to them. B said to keep it brief and to the point—tell them about the molestation by Dad and that Leah was molested, too. Reassure them that Alan and I love each other and we'll get through this and be stronger as a couple and as a family.

Sam came into the house and saw me upset and asked about me—I told him I was fine. He asked me later if I was upset at something he had done. Of course not, I told him and to never, ever think that. His words, his concern, made me realize we need to sit the kids down and discuss it as a family ASAP. It was time. I regret putting the kids and Alan through all of this but know that it was inevitable; only wished the meltdown had happened long ago. B has explained that everyone deals with trauma differently—some people face it soon after, others not until they are in their 60s. There is no timetable. So stop beating yourself up. Stop the critic in your head.

> Nov. 22 3:26 a.m.
> My bday gift to myself are bracelets that say:
> Be present
> Live in the moment
> This too shall pass
> She believed she could so she did

It helps to look at them on my wrist when I'm feeling unhinged.

Went to Millwood (*a small, scenic town on the Ohio River*) for two days. A relief to get away. We (*Alan and I*) both needed it, a diversion. Tired of feeling tired. Visualize myself telling the little girl in me that she will be okay, hugging her, wiping her eyes, parenting her. Makes me sick to think about what happened but if I don't feel the feelings what is the alternative? Bring it out into the light, deal with it, and then put it away, make it small. Just want to sleep for hours and hours and hours but insomnia still haunts me. Realize it's okay not to be okay for now. Ask myself can I do this? Survive this?

Nov. 23

Glad bday is over—not in the mood to celebrate. Calling hypnotist today for help with my insomnia, anxiety, and self-esteem/self-confidence. Praying that it helps. Health in mind, body, and spirit. Went to church and the quiet and prayerful space helped—left me with a feeling of peace. Think of the words "extremely dysfunctional" when B first said them it took me aback, felt defensive of my family a bit but also felt Aha Someone finally gets it! Understands. I finally understand and see it all clearly, as it really was. Acceptance.

Nov. 24 8:33 p.m.

I'm picking up on a pattern—after a therapy session I need to decompress by driving or watching TV. Sessions are draining still. Hard to put into words my feelings. Glad Alan goes to help me finish my sentences at times. The anxiety hums beneath the surface of my skin. PTSD = extreme anxiety. Time to do Yoga stretches.

Nov. 26 5 a.m.

Hypnosis session yesterday, left me feeling restored and recharged. Emotional—cried afterwards when the hypnotist and I discussed the part where I was visualizing myself looking into the mirror and seeing the real Kristene. Tears for what happened to her. That girl/woman in the mirror. Session was relaxing and left me feeling like a rag doll but this morning I am feeling a confidence that I have not felt in a long time and I am not as tense. The sleep I had was restorative. The hypnotist said it will take 21 days to get back to a regulated, normal sleep pattern of 7 to 8 hours a night. Have a CD to listen to that will help me with this. It was worth the $100. Concerned about being alone with the hypnotist but Alan was sitting right outside and I felt safe. I'm smiling because the indecisiveness I've been feeling is gone. Confidence. Good to feel it throughout my body. The deep fear is gone, too. Today is Thanksgiving and I am thankful for:

my spirituality, my family and friends, B, my life, my past experiences, the Survivor in me, the fact that I'm smiling as I write this, the medications that are helping me through this, my doctor, my humor, my laugh, my ability to adapt, my willingness to learn and grow, a good sleep when I have one, my education.

My prayer for today: that I may fully heal and enjoy life, love myself so I can fully love others, let go and let others live as they choose, free from any desire to control. Fill me with love, peace, hope, kindness and forgiveness today.

We had our family meeting with the kids—went well. I explained what had happened in a straight-forward way, cried some, but kept it simple. They seemed relieved that we finally addressed it with them as a family. I asked them if they had any questions and they said no then we sat around and talked, chatted, it was nice just the four of us, talking, sharing, laughing.

Nov. 27 1:32 p.m.

Still processing hypnotherapy session. Before the session, the hypnotist mentioned a woman who came to him for hypnosis because she thought she was molested by her father but she wasn't—felt angry when he said that—hyperaware and defensive of comments like this—I thought don't go there because I know what happened to me. Realized not to take a comment like that personally. He said something about how what comes out in hypnosis is not admissible in court—told him that is not why I'm here and my dad is dead. Know he was covering his bases. He didn't know what my goals were with the session. Told him I just wanted to sleep, to feel less anxious all the time, and to feel confidence again. The hypnosis was for me, for my health. Want my equilibrium restored. Crying now thinking about the part of the session when I felt uncomfortable looking in the mirror—seeing myself and how I feel now about myself, how it has changed how I see myself, my past. Why was I so sad when I remembered looking in the mirror, why do I have this feeling of disliking myself? The abuse took a piece, a part of me who needed parents to respect her, to love her and to protect her. I cannot change the past but I can love myself and the little girl inside me.

Nov. 29 9:02 p.m.

Realizing a pattern to this process—a trigger then tears/sobbing last night, sobbing overwhelming sadness, felt hot, then sick, then panic, next morning I am very, very down and dark thoughts, feeling of hopelessness. Even though intellectually I know I will get better and these thoughts are part of the depression, this dark thinking scares me. Part of me says fuck it, just disappear, I visualize a bottle of pills, taking them all, an alternative to this pain. A fix. Then I picture Alan and the kids and I don't think I would end my life but these thoughts surface and I hate it, hate all of this. The grief, the reality of my past, feel naked, exposed, engulfed in sadness. The cheerleader in me says what would you say to someone who is going through this? Keep going, don't give up it will get better. Bright, beautiful future ahead, so many good things in store for you. I can do this. I can live in the present. Trying hard to keep it together. I've already melted down, snapped, can it get any worse? I won't end my life but I'm left with dealing with what I need to. Alan held me last night as I cried and told him I feel like a freak, had that why-me feeling that makes me angry when it surfaces. I feel like I need instructions to live in the present. How do I do this? I know the answer: allow myself to feel sad, to grieve. Roller coaster of feelings.

DECEMBER

Dec. 1 12:55 p.m.

B reminded me to refer to what happened to me as a meltdown—a kinder, gentler word for psychosis. It wasn't a nervous breakdown. She said the words 'psychotic break' makes it sound more than it was. Remember everyone has meltdowns. Overwhelmed. What was it? Everything colliding—the knowing, the emotions—stunned me and my mind was flooded with all of it.

Dec. 2 6 a.m.

Feeling a great sense of peace, love and serenity this morning. Feeling joy at celebrating Sam's 21st bday. 21. My baby is going to be 21. Proud that he is my son. Love his sense of humor, his sensitivity, kindness, openness. He is his own person and I'm so proud of him for that.

Went to an Al-Anon meeting, has been over 10 years, since I've been to one. Sitting around the table hearing other people's stories helped me feel a peace of mind—not so alone in my pain. Working at not feeling shame, working on letting go of the memories and the feelings about my childhood. B said I'm the white sheep of my family and I know I should be proud of that and not feel guilty about it. Look at me! I am strong, smart, a survivor. I did not repeat the dysfunction that I grew up with.

Elizabeth and Sam had a better, stable childhood than me and I don't give myself enough credit for that. Let's start doing that Kristene. Be proud of how you chose a different path. Relax and let God do the work, handle it because my need for control over this just makes me anxious. Trying to run from my past caught up with me. Don't judge yourself anymore. I'm taking care of myself in healthy ways—spiritually, mentally and physically. Mindfulness. Communication—much better between me and Alan. I'm so fortunate for having the time and space to heal. My wish for 2016 is that I have peace, love, hope and moments of joy in 2016.

Dec. 4 5:24 a.m.

Had a dream with Dad in it—he was close to me, standing at my right, and glaring at me. Surrounded by darkness. Felt an absence of love, threatened, he was looking at me in a menacing way. Left me feeling uncomfortable. He was looking at me like a parent would look at a child in anger, disappointment, as if displeased with me. What had I done? When he died I cried, felt so sad for the loss of a parent, despite the abandonment, the lies, the continued disappointment my entire life. My whole life, I longed to have a father in my life.

Even when despair returns from flashbacks, dreams, memories, the long buried feelings, the sadness, the shame, the embarrassment he caused me, the desire to not exist, I know they are just feelings and I can move through them. I am strong enough to move through them and heal. At this moment, I feel myself moving beyond this. Today I will take that as a blessing. The feeling of I made it. I see and feel the pain and I can handle it. I will be okay. I look in the mirror and know I will be okay. I see little Kristene, curious, intelligent, creative, waving at me and smiling, telling me she's happy, telling me she loved the freedom she had as a child, the explorer she became. I see myself hugging her, giving her the blue blanket I bought and she's happy to take it, take back what was stolen from her, wrap herself in it and run off to play, to create, to feel safe, to feel powerful, and protected.

Dec. 7 5:06 a.m.

Happy 21st birthday Sam! Feeling clear-headed today. Started reading a book *Surviving Childhood Sexual Abuse* I had ordered in October but unable to read it until now. Had wanted to learn more, to have another guide through this but was afraid, felt sickened to even look at the two books I bought so I tucked them in the bookcase. Fits and starts that's how I feel at times about all of this.

Celebrating Sam's bday at the Miller Inn tonight. Teary thinking about how quickly he's grown—my baby. Feels like a dream at times, the past flew by, the present flying by wanting to catch hold of it and slow it down.

Working at living in the present, not letting my mind drift off, blank out, go to another place, overthinking. Don't want to miss all of the joys of watching this new phase of my children's lives, celebrating Alan and I having time to ourselves as well. Feels like I'm on a bridge looking one way at the past, and turning around to look forward to the future. Transitions never easy feels odd to let go to have this time to think about myself, to just exist. B said I'm doing what I'm supposed to do to heal—following her advice—that some patients go to therapy week after week and nothing changes for them. I don't want to stay stuck. I don't want to feel like a victim. I hate feeling sorry for myself but I do right now, or sorry for the little girl in me who was hurt. She deserves to have someone feel sorry for her. Trying to look both at my past; to heal and move on. It's confusing to me at times—all these feelings I'm experiencing like a ping-pong inside my head; the feeling that my chest is being opened and all of my feelings are gushing out, spilling onto the floor. Working on trust—that whatever happens in the future I trust I will be okay. Feel like a different person, like a veil has been lifted from my eyes, and I see the past clearly, for what it was.

Gratitude, gratitude, gratitude. Thank God for my life, for all that I have, for surviving all that happened to me because it made me who I am and I am proud of that.

Dec. 8 5 a.m.

Leah text and asked again about going to therapy with me. She said she's going to go on the 15th—hope she does. I'd like her to get help for herself, to hear her story, to help me continue to put the puzzle pieces together of that time in my life. Like me, she was trying to survive as a child living in a sick house. She turned her anger outward, I turned mine inward. We both suffer from depression and anxiety. Know now for the first time in my life that we share this common bond, have this connection, we are both survivors. Understanding, making sense of the past, her past and mine. How we were affected by the dysfunction, makes our behaviors as teenagers make sense, the choices we made. The few times I've talked to her on the phone lately, I've said I love you before hanging up and she's said it back. Never thought that would happen—that expression of love and warmth.

Today we move Elizabeth to her new house! So happy for her—relieved she will be close to her job and pray that she will continue to feel better, that her headaches will go away with this new medication. Praying also for Sam's health—he's sick with bronchitis and possible pneumonia. Wish he hadn't been sick on his bday. Will get results from chest x-ray today or tomorrow.

Now hope to go back to sleep before we get going to move Elizabeth.

Dec. 9 6:57 a.m.

Mental clarity. Feeling of peace. I was concerned about how I would get through Thanksgiving, the holidays. I made it through Thanksgiving, my favorite holiday, even though I wasn't feeling happy, I made it. Forced cheerfulness on my part. Ambivalent about Christmas. Looking forward to putting up the tree but it will be the first Christmas without a child living at home. Life. I always loved Christmas with the kids. No matter how bad things were growing up, Mom always made a point of giving us gifts we wanted. How difficult this must have been as a single mom, she worked so hard to keep a roof over our heads and gave us what she could. I admire her for that and I am grateful.

Trying to relax and honor my struggle—fully appreciate the lessons I learned from my past. Knowledge is wisdom. I felt safe enough for the meltdown to happen, the trapped feelings are out and I felt like I was at the end of a long, hard, long distance run, an exhausting race and I collapsed at the finish line. The meltdown is part of my journey—now I can love myself, like myself for who I am. Feeling like I've folded that knowledge into my body/my mind. Processed it and it is part of me and I'm okay with it. I was molested by dad at a very young age. He was a sick man. I can write those words and my past makes sense to me finally. I know what happened and it does not overwhelm me anymore. I no longer feel the urge to flee. I feel comfortable in my own skin again.

Tomorrow Sam is going to therapy with us. Concerned and nervous about it. What will be said? How will he feel?

Dec. 10 7:06 a.m.

Therapy session at 10 a.m. Anxious about it but not as much as I have been in the past. Need to let go of the outcome of the session. Sam is an adult and he is worried about me. Having him go to therapy will help him and that eases my tension. All of this will be less of a mystery to him. Will help him to understand.

Focusing on my healing, myself. Feels odd sometimes. I'm used to always focusing on something or someone else and now that I have time to myself while it feels good it also feels strange.

Put out Christmas decorations last night, tossed several in a bag for Goodwill. Feeling like starting fresh, throwing out the old, and beginning anew. Shedding the past.

Dec. 11 5:30 a.m.

Tough talking about what happened to me and what I'm going through with Sam in the room. B did a great job of explaining what happened to me and it was good for me to hear an overview of it; hear her explain how awful it was for me and how there was no one there to protect me. Feels like I finally have an advocate—someone who is here for me now, a parent to guide me through this when I feel as if I'm a lost little girl. Afterwards at lunch, I asked Sam if it helped him to understand why all of this had happened and he said yes. I told him if he ever wants to know anything or has any questions to just ask. He said he would.

At times when the critic in my head starts, the self-doubt, I remember I am an adult who makes wise decisions, who raised two children, who did the best she could, who gave them a better childhood than I had, who is tired, so tired, but keeps going. Yesterday was stressful and it zapped me. I'm feeling it fully now. I hate that the kids know what I went through. Wanted them to never know.

12/12 8:35 p.m.

Rough, rough day. After effects of a tough therapy session with Sam. Told Alan I'm tired of thinking of all of this—this loud, rowdy crowd in my head blocking out any sense, any feeling of normalcy, of the old me. Talking to him is another lifeline. Conflicted feelings today about dad, about having to FEEL this way. It hurts to feel. It's healthy but the little girl, the child within me, wants to run from it today. What else, what other memories are locked inside my mind? I want to know how long this deep hurt will last—had sobbing and panic attack today. One of my triggers is money and worries about it—need to STOP and think and I did. I recognized that money was the trigger and the source of the anxiety—money problems, the lack of money, when I was growing up and the panic, worry it left me feeling as a child and teenager. We are fine financially—farming has its cash-flow crunches and we are in one right now. Fortunate and grateful for all that we have and I know this crunch is temporary. I just had to talk myself through the panic. Not let the child who is fearful dominate my mind.

This despair today leaves me feeling like I've been run over by a truck—flattened. I want to rise above, to move on—all those ridiculous clichés clamor in my head. There is no rising above this, only healing and then living with it. I looked into the mirror this morning, really looked into my eyes and said to that woman "You were molested and you are okay. You will be okay. You are a survivor." Did I feel any better? Some. Some relief. I've been avoiding that mirror—the mirror in my hypnosis session—when I looked into it and saw myself and cried. Another connection made—looking in the mirror this morning and crying this afternoon. Meltdown. Lost it. Had a good, sobbing, snot running cry, rocking myself, felt sick. Thought of the quote "Wherever you go, there you are."

Name it. Say it. The truth. The sad, sick truth. I was hurt as a little girl in the most profound way but I do not/will not stay hurt. I will heal. I AM.

Dec. 14 6:32 a.m.

My entire life I have felt tense at some level, a coiled spring inside and for the first time I do not feel like that. A release has occurred. Relaxation inside and out—what a good cry does for me. Every cell, muscle, bone feels like it's free. Since September this mending has been taking place, through the pain, feeling it, a slow releasing of pain I've held deep inside. The body remembers what the mind forgets B says—the mind remembers and the body heals—the mind heals, wholeness, completeness. One-ness.

No longer feeling overwhelmed by the truth. It no longer leaves me feeling trapped. What happened, I won't let it kill my spirit, deaden it, I deadened a part of myself my entire life. I can't change what happened but I can choose to heal from it—allow that, accept, embrace the love and help I have. Accepting the unacceptable.

I can ask why me? And the answer is why not me? It happened to me, to my sister, to thousands and thousands of children, to innocents. And it still happens. Criminal.

Alan told me I am one of the strongest people he knows. I appreciated hearing that. I have to be strong, I have no choice do I? When I thought about taking my life I remember all that I have. Over and over those thoughts intrude, have been there since September. I need to remind myself that when I go there again, because I know I will, it's a roller coaster ride this recovery, I will come back from it. I pray I will always come back from it.

Right now I'm happy, not sad or despairing. I smile and do not feel like I'm dragging a weight around like I have felt my whole life; always staying one step ahead of something— now I know what that something was. The light shines on the darkness. The secret, the family secret, is now out. I know! I choose to walk in the light and the truth. A new beginning. A change. Rebirth. I am safe now. Remember I felt safe enough to remember what happened to me and that took courage and I can do this hard work of healing.

Dec. 15 1:07 p.m.

At session discussed my panic attack over letting worries about money overwhelm me when the reality is we are financially solid. B called it a thinking error. Knowing, understanding why I reacted as I did will help me to stop and think next time. Working not to catastrophize, this is a learned behavior from the past. Discussed mornings as the time of day I can struggle the most. B said my dreams, which have been jumbled and chaotic, could be bringing forth memories of the abuse. We talked about how mornings were most likely the time of day when dad abused me—he had the easiest access because mom was always at work early and he took me to daycare and later to school. Leah was going to go to this session but received a text at the last minute from her and she cancelled. Keep praying she will come to a session and begin her road to healing. I love her and want her to have the help she deserves.

B said to think of what happened to me as an avalanche I'm digging myself out of and as I continue to heal the ups and downs I feel eventually will even out and stay even. B complimented me and I need those words of encouragement and support so badly. She said look at all you've gone through and you're okay. I cried at those words, tears of relief, tears of acknowledging the painful past. She said I had bumps along the way but I made it and succeeded and I should be proud.

Still having some memory issues, trouble thinking of words or phrases at times. It's the avalanche that swallowed me and I need time to heal, dig out and I will be 100 percent in time, B said.

Working on naming my feelings, how I need time to process, to stop and think now.

A positive: stopped at the Knit Shop and I'm going to take a knitting class. Something I've always wanted to learn and it's relaxing and I will meet new people.

Today I'm washing all of Grammie's Noritake china that has been stored in the basement for years. Those precious pieces had dirt, mouse-droppings and newspaper stuck to them. Cleaning the pieces has been therapeutic; I see it as a metaphor for the struggles of the women, the dysfunction, in our family. Cleaning it, making it shine again, and displaying it in my dining room cabinet where it belongs. The dirt from the past washed down the drain.

Dec. 18 4:42 a.m.

Looking at the Christmas tree, lights, and gifts and feeling contentment—glad to be alive, glad to feel, to not just go through the motions like I was two weeks ago, was in a dreadful fog. It has lifted.

Dec. 23

At session yesterday I explained to B the guilt I've carried that Leah was the one beaten by dad and I was not. Or if I was I have no memory of it. She explained that predators use any excuse to molest so anything Dad could use as a reason to abuse Leah he did. I was not old enough to talk back like she did. Another piece to this puzzle—another piece that makes sense and I can now release that guilt.

Finally located our wedding album—had wanted to find it and take out the pictures dad was in and throw them in the dumpster. He was in three of them and I tore them into small pieces. Relief they are no longer in my home. Stared for a while at the picture of us before he walked me down the aisle. Recalled how I was nervous walking into the church and he told me just to hold on to him and that I would be okay. I had always appreciated that moment when he was truly there for me. Hesitated about throwing that picture out but realized if I held onto it, I would hang onto a falseness.

Throughout this process, the day after a therapy session has always been the roughest of the week but this "day after" has not left me feeling as wiped out—the best "day after" I've ever had. Next week's session will be rough because Elizabeth is going with us and it is painful for me, but necessary, for the kids to come to a session. I survived Sam going and I feel better that they have a deeper understanding of what happened to me, that I'm healing. That I'm still their mom—the mom they had always known disappeared for a short time but I am back and becoming healthier.

Dec. 24 5:05 a.m.
Gratitude list for today…thankful for:
1. My faith in God
2. My family
3. This awakening and the help I'm finally receiving.
4. My writing to heal

Feel a leveling out. A calmness within. Settling into this new person I've become. Feel an absence of that churning, constant anxiety inside—a TERRIFIC feeling I want to savor.

Dec. 27 5:54 a.m.
Thinking about PTSD. Know that it is a mental illness that is managed. I am doing everything I need to do to help myself—medications and therapy. Overthinking right now. Sam went out with friends and it triggered memories of the alcoholics in my life. He is not an alcoholic but thinking of him turning 21 and out drinking triggered these thoughts…
- Uncertainty about or worry about a loved one's drinking; feeling out of control
- When I was young being awakened by mom, drunk, telling me nonsensical things, hearing her voice, breathless, slurred words, darkness of night
- Feeling powerless at such a young age, confused, loss of control, no control, no boundaries

The freedom I had as a young girl because no adults were around, I liked it at times, but I paid a price. It made me independent, I had to be, at such a young age but it also left me vulnerable in other ways, physically and emotionally alone. I felt like I raised myself from the age of 12 on. Remember Kristene—you stopped the cycle. YOU did that.

Have been feeling, have had fears, of the future, of impending doom. PTSD symptom—I need to remember this. I do not want to live my life in fear. Stay positive. Positive. Positive. Wearing the Alex and Ani bracelet Elizabeth gave me for Christmas with the word Positive written in different languages on it. My talisman.

Gratitude for:

The positive qualities of Mom, grateful to have her still alive and a part of my life—no matter how little she can give of herself, what she can give I cherish.

Feeling less resentful these days. Feeling my spirits lift.

Peace, love, hope, wisdom and truth in my life.

Moving forward. Healing.

Dec. 30

My PTSD situational, not chronic PTSD like combat veterans experience. B explained this to me again—I remember her explaining this now in an early therapy session. Still need basic information explained to me at times. Hit the reset button. Elizabeth went to therapy today, emotional but I wasn't as nervous beforehand as I thought I would be. Felt natural she was there with us.

B said at least I'm not an angry and bitter person as I could have easily become. I had plenty of anger and I smiled over at Alan when she said this because he could be the target of it at times. But now I understand, we understand, why and where this anger came from. I'm happier now and Alan said he recognized this in me before I did. Reminding myself, as B said, not to let the scared little Kristene inside take over. Adult Kristene is in charge!

Dec. 31 6:06 a.m.

Warmth, contentment. Understanding finally I need to protect the little girl still inside who wants/needs/has to have the protection of a caring, loving, kind parent. Well she has it now.

2016 whatever it may bring, I know I will be okay. The Year of Fun as Alan and I are calling it, year of letting go, moving forward, making many more wonderful memories as we have always done over the years.

Picturing Elizabeth sitting on the couch between us in B's office. Comfort, security, love coming from the three of us. Elizabeth in the middle knowing we are there for her as we've always been. It brought another sense of closure to this therapeutic process as it did when Sam went with us. Having them see me go through the meltdown, the confusion and fear they felt, and then the healing process, the recovery, being a part of that, I hope they take away from it a sense that I am a strong person, who is working hard to get back to being myself, to get back to them. My prayer is that despite the turmoil inside me when they were growing up, the depression, the anxiety, they felt cared for, loved and protected. They felt they were a priority. It is my privilege to be their mom, to have raised them, to see them as wonderful adults, my hearts. They are of me and as I did from the moment they were born, I marvel at how amazing they are—perfect joy and love walking around in the world.

Gratitude for today:

I am walking through the fire and I am free from fear.

January

Jan. 1 2:40 p.m.

B talks about grief and my grieving the little girl who was hurt and the losses she has suffered and the part of me, the adult Kristene, who protected her and dealt with those losses in so many messy ways. I'm working at reconciling it all. Looked back at the calendar again trying to understand, seeing clearer the timeline of events leading up to the meltdown, remembering aha! Yes this happened, then that. On way home from lunch Alan and I discussed the timeline and he said the day of his treadmill test is when it happened. I remember being there with him, can see him on the bed, nurses, hooking him up but I was in a zone, fog-like, frozen state, emotionless, disconnected. I recall that clearly now. He said he called Dr. G that day and told her nurse that I was struggling, that something was off with me and that I needed to be seen as soon as possible. I looked back at the calendar. That day was Sept. 8, the day of his treadmill test.

This looking back, making sense of the timeline is helping me to reclaim those lost days. As if remembering them

I recapture, regain part of myself. Gain control. There's that word. Control. Wanting control even now of the uncontrollable. I saw Dr. G on the 9th and then B on the 15th for the first session. Those first few weeks on my medicine, such relief, for the first time I felt like I was in a protective bubble. Released from the frozen state, the fog of confusion, trapped, memory zapped, mind distorting reality. Zip, zap, gone. That is what the psychosis felt like.

Jan. 4 6:27 a.m.

The flashback I had the other night keeps coming to mind. Leah and I in a house, a house from our childhood, but empty, scary, a cold place. This intense fear, feeling of needing to escape an oncoming danger, knowing something bad was coming for us. Recognized the bad as a person—dad. It left me, leaves me, feeling shaken, fear lingers for days. Flashbacks stay with me; different from regular dreams.

My concerns today: when will I feel what? Back to myself? There is no going back to the old Kristene, I know that. I accept that now. When will this constant back and forth feeling of anxiousness, uncertainty, loss of confidence, loss of feeling secure end? Focus on recovery; any movement forward. Remember how far you've come, the acceptance you have now, the living with this realization, this knowing. I'm doing it and not falling apart. I'm living. I'm coping.

Jan. 18 4:41 a.m.

Feel back to square one. Yesterday was a rough day—woke up feeling like a storm raging in my head. Thought of that bottle of pills and swallowing them all just to have some peace, to rid myself of the pain. Had not been able to write for two weeks. Cried and cried. Alan held me and I told him I can't do this anymore. Finally told him how I was feeling, how the thought of killing myself was playing like a broken record in my mind at times, how I'd had this feeling on and off for a long time. Honesty.

Saw Dr. G last week. She said it's the grief and anxiety. My desire to escape it is causing this suicidal thinking. The numb, hopeless feeling is excruciating. Alan made me promise to call him when I feel that way again. Told me he and kids need me. I need them. Assured him I would never do that to them. At times, if it were just me, if I did not have them, the loneliness, pain, reality, ache overwhelms and I think I would do it, disappear, go, die. I need to feel gratitude again for my life, to know I will be okay, make it through this. I want to be on the other side of this. B and Alan remind me that I will. I will. I will. I will. Finally being honest about it with Alan was a release. Have not wanted to tell him, worry him, but I knew to move forward I had to tell him. Trust.

Praying to God to help me through this dark and lonely time—help me to see each day one day, one moment, one second at a time that I will make it. Survive this journey and feel the healing and lightness of spirit again for good. Keep going. Dr. G said in her experience it takes a year to recover from this trauma. PTSD will lessen as I get further away from it. She said I had built a house of cards in my mind to explain things to myself, to make sense of what happened to me, that my mind is complex. Now that the anxiety is gone, I don't know what to make of not feeling that way. It was my fuel. The anxiety is what kept me going. I WILL MAKE IT. September 2016 feels so far away but one day at a time and I will get there.

Jan. 19

Shared with B how I've been feeling—thoughts of ending my life. She made me promise and say it out loud that I would not do it. To value myself—to say what is good about me. She asked if I'd had those thoughts before and I said yes. I just never told her or Alan.

Affirmation: My life is worthwhile—it is worth living. I am an amazing person who has overcome many obstacles in my life. I have value and so much to look forward to. I will not give up.

B said the miracle is that I turned out as well as I did. That I am amazing because of that. God help me to see myself this way; to value myself.

I am to write another letter to Dad this evening before I leave town for a few days. Alan will read it out loud at therapy next week. Teary and emotional and feel like a rock is on my chest. Want these cold, gray days to go by quickly.

Gratitude for today:

My life

My family

Every breath I take

Jan. 20

Acceptance that healing takes time. I'm in this fight and I will win. The darkness will pass and I will come through this healed and whole. See myself stepping into a healing stream and floating along, knowing the rough, turbulent waters won't last.

Jan. 25 5:30 a.m.

Yesterday was the first time since the psychotic break I woke up feeling "normal"—settled, content, peaceful. Relief from the chaos inside. Realized I've been living in fear my entire life to a certain extent. These past few months it has intensified—fear of loss of control, about unknown future, old fears from the past can overwhelm. I can let those go now. I have been safe for a long, long time and I can now truly live that way. I'm safe. As Alan continues to remind me, I'm letting out 47+ years of stuff and it is going to take a long time to heal.

In session it made me happy to hear B say that I will always be angry at dad—good to know—it's a feeling I want to hang onto. I always have been angry at him but I stuffed that emotion among many others.

Jan. 26 5:48 a.m.

Gratitude today for the truth.

Jan. 27

At therapy yesterday Alan read the letter I wrote to dad and then we took turns tearing it up. Burned it when we were home—cathartic process.

January 28 5:30 a.m.

Slept with my blue blanket last night—had calmer dreams. I was in a strange place with people I did not know and I was at a counter or office for some procedure? Or test? B. said to hold blanket close when sleeping—my comfort—to grow the child within. This blanket has helped me reclaim the innocence taken from me. The hurt and scared little girl is going to grow up.

Elizabeth invited me to see a show at Collins Theater Saturday night—a musical about LGBTQ community telling their stories—will be touching and emotional.

Taking nothing for granted anymore. Savoring, fully living life.

Gratitude today for my sister.

Remember each day I breathe I am healing and growing. God help me work at forgiving dad for my own well-being, otherwise what happened has power over me. Very sick people molest their children and my dad was one of them. For eternity he is paying for what he did to us and while that gives me comfort it does not give me pleasure. Nor should it. It's all so tragic. Pain is anger and I want less pain—praying for calmness, maturity, love and release to replace the pain.

February

Feb. 1 4:24 a.m.

Had lunch with Leah the other day and she told me she saw a psychiatrist and is now taking an anti-depressant. Said she's feeling better—she was in a dark place and had been for some time. She told me she's been suicidal on and off for years. She looks better and she said she made an appt for Wed. with B. Praying she keeps it and continues to go. She's struggling to not start using again. She wants to self-medicate and if she does she'll go down that devastating road again. I told her to stay on her medication and to go to therapy once a week. Leah said she's not sure if she's going to tell mom she saw a psychiatrist and I told her not to but that's up to her—mom is incapable of being supportive. Leah said when she told mom she wanted to kill herself she received a cold response. Sick person living with a sick person. I'm supportive of Leah and will check on her but that's all I can do—and pray for her.

I'm still at times going through the motions of living. When will I look back on this as another obstacle I've overcome? Distance. Time and distance.

Feb. 2 6 a.m.

Sense of peace, contentment and accomplishment this morning. Good feeling not to deal with triggers, flashbacks and feelings of defeat. Defeat—a thinking error. Feeling powerless at times—a thinking error. In a stretch the past few days of feeling strong, empowered, positive.

Worked in office (*our home office*) going through January's receipts—up with the dogs and could not go back to sleep. Therapy today and my mind can still be on overdrive on days I have a session. This past Saturday I felt down and teary but minor compared to the week before. As B assured me the low dips will be less and less and I will even out. Acceptance about molestation—feel free of obsessive animosity toward dad—anger yes but not one that dominates my mind.

The break—"my bucket overflowed." Realize I not only had to accept abuse happened but had to accept loss of control of my thoughts and actions as a result of the break. Peace of mind. Gratitude for:

Knowing who I am and what I've been through
Boundaries
Hope

Feb. 4

Thinking errors, cognitive distortions, on my mind. Thinking error—my life has changed for the worse; I won't come back from this. Reality—I'm healing. I know the truth. I can finally heal and that is GOOD and healthy. Thinking error—suicidal thinking; giving up; my life not worth living anymore. Reality—my life is wonderful and I have so much to offer and many great adventures in store for me. I am looking forward to the future. The pain will not swallow me. I am healing. It takes time.

Had a dream two nights ago—one of my "knowing" or "truth" dreams where I come away with another piece of the puzzle. One that furthers my healing, understanding. It was vivid, crisp, real. I went to the store looking for dad. (*My father opened a small business when I was five and this was the store in my dream. Financially it never succeeded and it closed when I was in the 5th grade, age 11, when my parents separated. This business was always a source of tension between my parents and I would later learn my father borrowed a significant amount of money from my grandmother, his mother-in-law, to open it and never repaid her. It was also were he employed and began an affair with a girl who was a senior in high school. I learned about it through the rumors and a cruel comment by a classmate. I always felt sorriest for Leah who was a freshman and attended the same high school as the girl my father was involved with.*) Inside it was rundown, plain, stripped bare, holes in the walls. Some young people were sitting on a ragged couch, laughing and I asked where dad was because he was supposed to be there. More laughter as a young guy told me he wasn't there and hadn't been. I was confused by the look of the place and that dad wasn't there. The letter I wrote dad triggered this dream. I was "seeing" my dad was not who I thought he was. In the dream he was not at the store like he was supposed to be just like in my life, he was supposed to be there for me but he wasn't. He was not the dad I thought I had before my parents divorced. Truth dream.

At session B said again how well I'm doing and that it will take two years for this new dimension of my life, this knowing, to settle in my soul, fold or integrate into my being. She said to challenge the thinking errors when they surface, to write them down, because thoughts can be fleeting. My big thinking error at times is that I could have controlled the psychotic break or that I should have been able to control it. Correction: it was a natural outcome of what happened to me. The rush of memories were inevitable because I had gone as far as I could. It was in the natural course of events—a part of who I am now. While I will always be sad about what happened to me it won't be so overwhelming that it keeps me from feeling happiness and joy. I will always be angry, as I should be, about the abuse but I will not hang onto resentment and bitterness because that only hurts me, and I've hurt enough, and it keeps me unhappy and unhealthy.

Gratitude today for the gift of remembering.

Feb. 6 6:11 a.m.

Feeling more centered this a.m. not like yesterday. No strange, disturbing dreams. Worked in the office yesterday but felt like doing little else. Have not had teary days this week except at therapy on Tues. Going every two weeks now—feel confident this is what I need. The anxiety and sadness are here to stay whether I go every week or every two weeks. Feel more in possession of myself—less unhinged. Yesterday was down but not as low as I had been, just a slight dip in my mood. Finding comfort in the small things: my soft, blue blanket, reading, the dogs, watching TV, writing, breathing, existing.

Floating along in this current of sadness, anger, contentment, discontentment, acceptance, love, and being here now. Has been weeks since I've felt like I've disassociated, drifted off. Can say I've felt numb on and off, feel apart from others. I guess that is the isolation, maybe disassociating? It's hard to see myself as I really am. Facing reality is difficult but an opportunity to grow. Painful but growth, truth, reality, necessary. Appreciate my life and even the rough times and struggles as they have made me strong even when I feel weak I know that is a part of this process. A renewal, a rebirth. My life is a blessing and what happened to me was a crime but it will not hold power over me and defeat me. I'm healing and moving forward. My life is valuable and worth living. I've crossed the threshold from darkness into light. It may feel dim at times but it is light nonetheless and I'll take it and feel grateful.

Feb. 9 6:54 a.m.

Picked up the *Courage to Heal*—needed to start reading it again—rough day yesterday. I can feel so hopeful at one moment and then boom in the depths of despair in another. Still accepting this healing process and the timing. It takes time and there's no rushing it. The pain, the heartache, the exhaustion will end or lessen to where it doesn't flatten me—make me withdraw and want to disappear. The emotional pain is so visceral, so severe, it feels like I can't bear it but then I think I have been all these months and I will continue to make it through. Reading *Courage to Heal* makes me cry—brings pain to the surface, helps release it and while it is painful it is necessary so I can fully live. I'm a different person now. No therapy this week and I'm doing okay with knowing this. Feel need today to withdraw into myself, to heal, lick my wounds. Prayer helps, so does watching movies, slowing down, taking each day as it comes. Working at being proactive, watching, thinking of what could trigger my anxiety and working through it ahead of time or learning what to do when it overwhelms me. Keep moving forward and loving myself. Remember my life is about today, not the past, not what happened to me then but today and healing. I'm in a good place with people who love me and protect me. I am working at letting go of my worries and fears.

Feb. 10 4:52 a.m.

Realized my focus on why dad molested me and Leah is pointless and keeps some of the focus of my recovery on him instead of my healing. As B said in the beginning, I'll never know why. He was sick. Period. I can let go of asking why. Healing is about ME and he is in the past. Nothing to me now. I have the answer to why I am the way I am—my behaviors in the past—and that is a gift to remember, to finally know. I am stronger than what was taken from me.

Feb. 11 6:16 a.m.

Feeling more grounded and less lost this past week. Today I have gratitude for:
God
My life—the past and present
Ability to adapt, reason, change
Love
Healing

Strength and hope

Courage

Not giving up

Peaceful, calm moments

Read in *Courage to Heal* that it can help to get in touch with the inner child, the hurt little girl inside me, the one who felt lonely and abandoned, by writing to her. I'm right-handed so I will write as the adult with my dominate hand and as the little me with my left hand. So here goes:

It's okay to be angry and sad, you should be.

Okay. I was confused and really mad at the way mom and dad acted. It hurt.

I know it did. You were hurt. You deserved to feel this way. But I am here for you now. Really here. No one can hurt you like that anymore. You are an amazing little girl and young woman.

I only wanted parents who didn't scare me and who were normal and I wanted a sister who was there for me. I wanted to be close to her.

You deserved to have those things but your family was very sick—very dysfunctional—they did not know how to be better parents. They did the best they knew how to do even though it fell far short of good parenting. You were not protected and you were a precious child, full of life, creativity, innocence, wonder, curiosity, and you deserved better. I know you wanted an older sister who was your friend and ally but she was hurt, too, and surviving like you in a difficult situation. Does this make sense to you? I know it is quite a bit to take in and understand.

I don't like it but I understand.

Remember there were good things about your childhood. People who loved you and cared for you the best they could. Grammie, Grandpa and Grandma—remember how they watched over you? They did not know how bad things were and what dad was doing. They were also doing the best they could. Relationships are complicated. Life is complicated.

I remember good times. I liked playing outside and feeling freedom. I could never trust the good times to last. There was always bad around the corner.

I know and I'm sorry you had to experience that. But that is over. You can trust that good times are not going to be followed by bad times anymore. You have the grown up me to watch over you and I'm a good parent. I love you very much. You are a beautiful, kind, creative child of God who deserves the best. You can trust me. I am here to take care of you and I will never leave your side even when you feel lost and lonely I am here. Please always remember that.

I will. I get scared and want to run, to disappear.

It is natural for you to feel this way. You were hurt deeply—it is normal for you to have felt this way your entire childhood but now that I'm watching over you, now that I know what happened to you—all of it—you don't have to run or disappear because you are finally free—free to be a little girl again. To stay that little, innocent girl inside. The adult me is all around you protecting you every second of every day. I love you and I want you to love yourself again. Do not run away. Do not disappear. Promise me you won't do that anymore. Promise me you won't hate yourself or get angry at other people when you are really angry about something from your past because that part of your life is over.

I promise. I trust you. You are honest with me and not lying. I know what to expect from you.

Good. I'm glad you feel this way. I want you to be happy and content. You are finally safe.

Feb. 13 11:16 a.m.

Have found myself less anxious, much, much less. I've stopped fighting my feelings. There's a calmness to my sadness now. What is next for me? I don't know but I'm through with thoughts of ending my life. The pain is still there and lessened and while I know the intensity will fluctuate I know I can talk to Alan and B about it. The molestation is part of my story, shaped my history, but so did many positive experiences. I have made many good choices in my life and I will not let what happened to me keep me down—I will not disappear, end my life because of the pain. My life is too valuable.

Feb. 16 5:44 a.m.

Had a sobbing cry last night. Has been a while since I had one of those. The pain, sadness build up and then I'm able to release it. Tears and more tears. It's only been six months since the meltdown Alan reminds me. Look how far I've come in that time. This is not hopeless. I will make it through this. I am strong. I want to live and enjoy life again. My simple prayer for today: Thank you God for all that I have. Peace. Love. Hope.

Feb. 18 2:05 p.m.

Unsettling dreams last night. Woke up feeling fearful and anxious. Did go to a CASA meeting last night and listening to other volunteers talk about the issue going on in their cases brought on flashbacks like lightbulbs going off pop, pop, pop— domestic violence, drugs, alcohol issues, all too familiar. At last session, B said that while I will be celebrating the anniversary of dad's death I'm still grieving and my body is reminding me of that today. The dreams brought on anxiety and uncertainty not as extreme as in the beginning but the feelings are still hovering. Told B my big thinking error is that the psychotic break was a huge setback in my life. She said to reframe it. It is a bonus because I know what happened to me and that it happened to my sister. Have felt more hopeful and noticing improvement in my mood and the feeling that I have been defeated by this is passing. Sometimes I want more memories of the abuse to surface and other times I'm frightened by the thought. I know they are in the back of my mind I just don't want to rummage around too much to find them. Feel that my mind has closed the door on them. I am learning to feel comfortable with this knowing.

Feb. 23 10:30 a.m.

Cold but beautiful blue sky today. Today the truth feels bearable. Another shift has occurred. Another day. Another opportunity to heal. Hopeful feeling continues. Keep going. You are a survivor and that's what survivors do. Live bravely.

MARCH

3/2 10:35 a.m.

Reflecting on how far I've come since September—grateful to be in a stable, safe place right now. I've decided I'm going to accept each day where I am emotionally even if it's a low point—this too shall pass.

Had dinner last night with Elizabeth and Sam. Sitting across from them felt good. It's been a while since the three of us went somewhere. Cherish those moments. While I still feel uneasy around them at times since the meltdown—I feel anxious about how they feel about me or what they think of me. I know I don't have to feel this way, or shouldn't feel this way, as Alan reminded me a few months ago they are smart and they understand what happened to me and why and that I had no control over the psychosis. I stopped feeling like I needed their forgiveness. They are so amazing and wonderful and mature. We are blessed to have them as our children. Let go of the shame of having had a psychotic break—that nasty thought still intrudes from time to time. Remember it's a bonus that I know what happened. Wishing things were different is futile. All I have is today and I need to stop looking at the past and focus on where I am today and hope for the future. All is well. Forgive yourself for wanting to give up in January. I'll never forget that feeling—since September it was the first time I felt that way in mind, body and spirit. This overwhelming desire to not exist because I was in so much pain. My overcoming this and thriving is my victory. I wanted to give up but I didn't. I had Alan and B telling me not to and the image of Elizabeth and Sam appeared in my mind each time I would go there.

Allow myself to feel all of my feelings—happiness, sadness, joy, fear, lonely, numb, indifferent and on and on. And anger. It's okay to be angry—I have a right to be! I don't have to pretend anymore. When I feel overwhelmed take baby steps. Cry. Keep going.

3/6 3:05 p.m.

Cathartic session with B on Thursday—many tears and working on positive inner dialogue. She said that I did nothing wrong to cause the molestation. It happened because dad was sick. Needed those words.

Longing to feel happy, carefree, relaxed in my own body. B assures me this will happen again. Not my fault. I may not like the sadness and fear and feeling so desolate and turned inside out but remember it's all bonus time. As B says it's incredible I have done as well as I have. I am proud of that—finally I can say it. I am deeply hurt, sad, and angry because of it but I am okay. I promise myself and I promised B that I will not harm myself even if that thought flits across my mind I will let it go past. I do not want to disappear. I want to be here for all the wonderful adventures ahead. I am more powerful than what was done to me.

March 13 1:35 p.m.

Florida was heavenly—beach, salt, sand did us both good. Alan's knees stopped aching and we spent the days at the beach reading, walking and then eating out every evening. I had a meltdown the night before we left. I had been thinking of the last time we'd been to Florida together—last February and all that has happened since then. It overwhelmed me. I just get so damn angry about all of it. When I caught myself going to that self-blame/hate-myself place I remembered B's words: You did nothing wrong.

Woke up feeling fearful—dreams left me this way. In one, a great tidal wave was coming at me and Alan. He was so calm and held my hand and told me it would be okay. I was terrified and trembling. Each day I say thank you God for Alan.

I am working at recognizing my thinking errors and correcting them. Why do I beat up on myself? Hold emotions in? My default setting was to stuff the hard things, not communicate, not trust. I'm hard-wired that way as I've learned all sexual abuse victims are. I still feel shell-shocked from it all from time to time as in "pinch me" this past seven months really happened? Just keep going. You have done it all of your life, day by day by day, and now is no different. Just breathe and heal.

March 18

Had a dream I was selected to assassinate this man who had done something evil (dad obviously). I was standing in this aisle and people were all around me sitting on benches or pews and the man was tied to a post. I raised a shotgun, or a bow and arrow, I can't recall now which one, but I had my arms up aiming and then woke up before I shot him. I knew the man was going to die. I remember thinking in the dream Why was I selected? I wasn't upset at having to kill him. In fact it was empowering and liberating.

I still struggle with forgiving him. So guess that means I haven't forgiven him and that's okay. B says I will someday. Do I need to forgive him to fully heal? Maybe. Maybe not. Working toward forgiveness, when I choose to do that, is part of healing. It means dad has no more power over me—the abuse has no power over me. It doesn't mean I let him off the hook. I acknowledge he was sick. Only a very sick person molests children. He had a choice and he chose to abuse. He chose not to get help for himself.

Remember faith instead of fear.

March 19 6:33 a.m.

Hard time falling asleep last night and up again early thinking. Going to Elizabeth's today to take her lawn mower to her that Sam fixed and we are going to help her tear out some bushes.

Cried some last night over what I'm going through—this huge life change that I didn't have a say in. Crying because I miss Elizabeth being closer to home. Faith not fear. Trusting

God and his plan for me is hard at times as if I need to constantly practice it—have faith in having faith. Gratitude I do have. This meltdown left me doubting myself and trusting myself. Remember: this truth is a bonus.

Elizabeth and I leave for Florida in seven days woot woot! Love our mom/daughter trips. Need to go to bookstore for my beach reads.

Also woke up concerned about Sam and this cold/cough he's had on and off all winter. Just worry about my children and always will. Remember all is well. God has all of us in the palms of his hands.

March 21 1:51 p.m.

Dr. G had to reschedule the appt. I had today—didn't want to go anyway. Told Alan last night I feel embarrassed going. I know I shouldn't (thinking error) and he reminded me of this but I do. Sad and teary thinking of all of this. Push through those thoughts. The sun is out. It's cold but I worked in the yard for little bit and that helped. The embarrassment feeling is a thinking error. I had no control over the meltdown—all that came out—I don't even remember all of it but I remember the things I never wanted anyone to know—my secrets—and I felt, still can feel at times, so exposed. That's a thinking error too. Alan reminds me it's healthy that everything, all the past memories, are out and intellectually I know this but at times the sadness, the tears, the bits of shame still present, all overwhelm me. Thinking error—shame.

Last night I told Alan how I feel odd inside like I'm missing a piece of myself, a large part of myself I want to fill up with something. It's the absence of anxiety—like a steam engine inside I had frantically shoveled coal into my entire life until now. I am still—will I ever stop?—trying to figure out how to live with this. I know I will I just have to talk myself out of the funk. I am feeling mentally stronger and more stable. Focusing on trying to lose weight. Anxiety has affected my appetite. I'm either wanting to eat or thinking about snacking to fill up with something or I am frightened about gaining more weight. My issue with control. I need to control what I'm eating and how much—I need to control something so I am dedicating myself to losing weight.

I have so much to be grateful for—I'm feeling my feelings instead of shutting down and shutting people out. I can let my guard down at times.

As Alan said we will make it through this like we made it through the year Elizabeth had her back surgery.

Your past is in your past Kristene even though it reared its ugly head last September it is PAST. Do not let it dominate your days and rob you of your present. It's taken enough. Now it's bonus time. Life is good. Truth is out. Be present. Live in the moment. Right now the moment is good. All is well. I have a newfound sense of peace inside me now and it will take adjusting to but this is what healthy feels like.

March 25 12:01 p.m.

I've been working on not filling my days, my insides, with other people or activities so I can avoid my feelings and thoughts. The engine inside me has slowed and I'm more comfortable with myself these past few days.

Had dinner with Patty last night—nice spending time with her. Sitting in a restaurant talking, eating, feeling normal and connected with my friend. She asked how I'm doing and I told her much better finally, finally feeling as though the worst is behind me. The intense feelings—shock, anger, deep sadness, suicidal thinking, are not as often or intense. I'm glad she asks because each time I talk about it with her I feel less like I have something to hide. Enough hiding.

APRIL

April 2 3:45 p.m.

Sam is asleep on the couch—not feeling well. He became sick while Elizabeth and I were in Florida. If he's not better by Monday I'll call the doctor.

At the beach one day this past week I was looking at the water and thought how I could describe what it felt like to have a psychotic break—the image of my head being zipped open and all of my thoughts tumbling out onto the sand while I desperately tried to hang onto reality, routine each minute of the day. The sense of numbness, of floating through time detached from the world as it went on around me. I was part of it yet I wasn't. As the saying goes time heals all things or at least makes them bearable. I'm hoping for the former.

April 5 3:00 p.m.

Feeling confident today and I love this feeling—the old me. Enjoying the day and the sun. I'm 8 months into this healing process. Working on my positive inner dialogue.

Working to stay mindful of doing it. Feeling alive instead of feeling like a walking ghost.

I'm working on letting go of negative feelings around anything related to my meltdown. Shame, regrets, what others think of me who know what happened. B said, it's another dimension to me. And she smiled when she said it. It's a good thing that I know! It's another piece of my story. I'm a good person. I did nothing wrong. Attack those negative thoughts that creep in.

I'm concerned about Sam. He has an ultrasound Thursday a.m. Hope we have some answers that day or Fri. and then a plan to get him well. Concerned about his low blood count but know that means his body is fighting an infection somewhere. He will heal and be well again. Positive thinking. Positive inner dialogue.

April 17 10:36 a.m.

Elizabeth turned 26 yesterday. The four of us had dinner last night. The years have flown by and I love having her home this weekend. Sam has his gallbladder out this coming Wed—he'll be pain free!

I'm tapering off Risperdal finally. Did not like how it made me feel. Saw Dr. G on Friday. We talked about what happened and she asked if it was my dad who molested me and I said yes. She said she figured out I was molested by someone when I was little based on how I described my reaction to the molestation in the pool.

It's a relief to put all of the pieces together and make sense of my past and present.

Dr. G praised Alan and said how much he loved and adored me. She said he is a good, solid man and she wanted to poke him to see if he were real because she rarely sees that in a man lol! She said at the initial visit, he had tears in his eyes a few times as the stories from my past tumbled out. It never occurred to me to share the deepest, darkest parts of my childhood with him. I wanted to forget them and never have to face them again. Ha.

I told Alan what she had said because he is all that—he is my rock and if it weren't for his support through this it would be an even bigger struggle to heal and our marriage could have fallen apart. This has brought us even closer together, more than we've ever been, because a barrier has been broken, a wall that existed because of the anxiety, the hidden truths, my state of mind before the meltdown. How could the sexual abuse not affect the most important relationship I have? I am so grateful to have him and this life.

I did nothing wrong. I have forgiven myself. I am a good person. I did not deserve to be molested. I survived the best I could in an extremely dysfunctional environment. I was denied a childhood but I provided one for my children. I am strong. I am proud of myself and proud of surviving. One day at a time—as Alan reminds me, "Another good day." I've been having good days consecutively and God I am so grateful for that. For the first time in my life, I have let go and I can work at living free from the hold of the past. My PTSD symptoms have lessened and add that to my gratitude list. I am no longer swimming upstream or treading water. I am swimming.

April 21 3:03 p.m.

Teary and feeling down again—sadness and fear triggered by the scent of stale cigarettes on the man who walked by me at CVS (*pharmacy*). He smelled like my dad. I paused after he passed and said to myself 'He smells exactly like Dad did." Ugh and ick.

Sam came home from lunch and I talked with him for a while. He's lying down now—still sore and tired from surgery. I felt the sadness come over me and I let it out— sobbing, feeling frozen, immobile, just want to curl up on the couch with my blanket and stare at the TV. I know tapering off Risperdal is playing a part in the intensity. B said I would be more emotional—another band aid coming off. I hate this helpless feeling I have—feelings of regret that all of this happened, where I am now, the meltdown and how it has left me, how remembering and recovering leaves me feeling. I'm better and healthier but this grieving the past is rough business. This is temporary. I've come so far in 8 months and I will only keep improving. Today just feels like a setback. I'm having a dip that's all. Smelling the cigarette smoke on that man, who also physically resembled my dad, was an unwelcome tug from the past.

April 22 10:54 a.m.

Alan took a walk with me last night and I talked to him about the trigger. I go from feeling positive to, while not feeling hopeless anymore, feeling down. The see-saw. I do not want to go back to suicidal thinking. It was a struggle to make it through that time and I'm afraid my mind will go back there.

I know my life has value—it's a thinking error to feel otherwise. My challenge is the fear that comes over me and is paralyzing. Faith instead of fear. Writing this out I can feel the anxiety lessening. I need to trust more: in God, in myself, in B. Look what I survived!

My gratitude list for today:

My spirituality

My family

Healing

My friends who check in on me.

April 23 2:13 p.m

Feeling like Rip Van Winkle who fell asleep for years and woke up to a changed world. This whole damn thing makes me sad and angry. Grief. Grief. Grief. I try to come up with some profound statement about what I'm going through and I can't—I can only say this really sucks. I've lived my life not knowing this awful truth and it feels like I am just now let in on a sick, cruel joke. I'm angry! I want to feel joy in my life again. I'm battling thinking errors right and left again; the ups and downs are back. I looked up quotes on the topic of memory and found this one that inspires me today:

"What if I've forgotten the most important thing? What if somewhere inside me there is a dark limbo where all the truly important memories are heaped and slowly turning into mud? The thought fills me with an almost unbearable sorrow."

I remembered because it was time for me to remember. I was supposed to remember. See it as a gift from God because it is. I've been given the gift of truth and that is beautiful.

April 26 1:09 p.m.

Therapy today at 3—feeling the usual nervousness I have before an appt. What will come up? What will we talk about? Maybe if I cry now I won't cry as much in therapy. Why I care who knows? It's the control—control my emotions—stuff my feelings. A habit.

I read how survivors don't have a fluid narrative about their childhood but instead bits and fragments because of the trauma. I spent my childhood ducking and dodging the chaos. My best memories from my childhood are playing outside, hanging out with friends, being at school and, as a teenager, dating Alan—he made me feel stable and safe. I was attracted to what I did not have in my life. Being outside, at school, anywhere was preferable than being at home. I have happy memories, of course. I was on my own for the most part after the divorce and I am independent because of this and I am strong. The avalanche that swept over me is over and I am digging my way out. I am on firm ground and feeling clarity—more like myself but better, the real me, not my pretend normal. I'm learning to be okay with all of this still and that's related to shame—the cycle I go through. I feel shame and then I self-talk my way out of that feeling. It's an old feeling from childhood—a thinking error.

April 27 1:39 p.m.

At therapy yesterday B said I am reordering my life and I am stronger and better than ever. I wrote this on a sticky note and put it in my daily planner. Words that help me make sense of what I'm going through. We discussed the flashback of smelling the cigarette smoke. B asked what the tears were telling me. Memory of what he smelled like during the abuse. Deep, deep well of emotion. Tears I couldn't stop for four days. Cathartic cry. Tears from long ago trapped inside me.

B reminded me of the grief cycle. I will return to depression, sadness, acceptance, and the feeling at times of "Did this all really happen to me?" referring to the break/ awakening and these past months of grieving.

She reminded me again of the importance of positive inner dialogue so I tell myself everything will be okay...I am a good person...I am strong...I did nothing wrong....all is well. I am making myself, forcing myself at times to reflect, think, and feel about what happened to me. Not go, go, go to avoid feeling. So much has happened in less than a year and it boggles my mind at times.

MAY

May 9 3:07 p.m.

Risperdal withdrawal still kicking my butt—yesterday was Mother's Day and I loved that the four of us had lunch together. Anxiety was through the roof though. Part of the anxiety and sadness was the lingering feelings of guilt I still carry about the meltdown and putting Elizabeth and Sam through it—I hate that they had to see me that way—know what I went through growing up. This seems ridiculous now that I've written it down but the mother, the protector in me, still wants to shield them from it. They are fine, they get it, so move past this. This is part of my story and they know it and they are dealing with it just fine as Alan reminds me.

While I can have a love/hate relationship with the meltdown, I am glad now that I know the truth. As B said I fought a battle at home and I survived terrible things and yet I rose above it and thrived. I am proud of that. I hope my children are proud of me.

I'll take this day with no sobbing and celebrate because today has been a GOOD ONE.

May 10 5:16 p.m.

Session with B was productive. She asked if I've reached clarity yet since withdrawing from Risperdal and I feel like I have—feel more like my old self. Therapy today left my insides feeling scrubbed clean. B said all of my issues over the years stem from the molestation and the pain it caused—wherever there is pain there is anger she reminded me. I'm working at letting out the anger.

B said to cry when I feel like crying don't stuff the tears anymore—release it all. Cried all through therapy—my safe place—and it felt wonderful such a release. B also reminded me to watch the paranoia. Don't question myself so much or worry what other's think about me. The paranoia—how is it related to the molestation? My covering up, hiding, being afraid of people finding out what went on at home. I'm so used to being "on guard" my entire life paranoia and anxiety are the natural outcomes of this. I can be so convinced I know what others are thinking or imagine their thoughts because I had to walk through landmines, tread carefully, try to figure out how to navigate the chaos at home. What's the mood going to be today? What will or won't happen? How can I turn crazy into something "normal?" Look normal, be normal, fit in.

B said I blocked the memories of the molestation all these years while Leah remembered them and acted out and numbed herself with drugs as a way to cope. I coped by blocking and pretending normal.

Prayer for today for clarity, wholeness, health.

May 28 4:48 a.m.

Back to the past...woke up at 3 unable to fall back asleep so I came downstairs and knitted. Anxiety. Anxiety. B explained in last session anxiety is embedded in me since childhood because of molestation—of not knowing what would happen and when. I will always have anxiety and PTSD but it is more manageable now. Today is Leah's bday and, weather permitting, she, mom and my nieces are coming over to swim and have lunch. This has me on edge. Christmas was the last time we were all together. Mainly, or primarily, or most definitely it's mom coming over that's making me anxious. She doesn't know what happened to me—any of it the meltdown, the molestation unless she does and is in deep, deep denial about it. The anger and sadness and anxiety about what happened colors how I feel about her—the veil has lifted and everything has changed for me. As B said, I've gone through a life-changing experience and nothing will ever be the same for me again. I'm working at acclimating myself to this. I'm working through a lifetime of issues in a short span of time and B said I'm handling it well—doing fine— not pretending everything is great and then having relapses. Knowledge is power.

May 31 9:20 a.m.

Had a satisfying dream—Dad was on the run because he was a criminal and he was finally caught. Woke up feeling relieved and fell back to sleep and dreamed I was lost in a big city, walked into a department store, and ended up being sexually assaulted. Woke up feeling scared, shaken. Feel nauseated and cold, out of sorts, anxious.

Had a cathartic wailing cry yesterday a.m. soothed the little Kristene in me. Painful to feel those feelings but that pain and those cries inside me won't be ignored anymore. I'm ready for the day when I will wake up and not feel anxious and will look forward to each and every day instead of feeling anxiety or depression or both. Maybe I'm coming down with something or maybe I'm just going to have a shitty morning. Remember the body remembers what the mind forgets. This weekend with family left me drained. Major trigger. Lethargic and unmotivated. No desire or energy to even knit and that is not like me.

JUNE

June 3 9:22 a.m.

B said she wants me to wake up looking forward to each day—have a mental list of positive plans for the day so I can enjoy it. Positive inner dialogue. I am working at actively using this first thing in the morning. I am rearranging my life and it takes time. B also said to work on my inner child so I can release all the intense sobbing out, to hold my blanket and rock if I needed to. To talk to her and tell her it will be okay so she can grow to a point where she is able to handle what happened to her. I visualize a silhouette of a grown woman with a small child inside curled up scared, hurting, crying—fear and sadness. I picture this woman (me) reaching down, picking her up and holding her, rocking her, telling her it's okay. No one can hurt her ever again. I am rooted to the ground and strong. I am better because I know the truth. I can put my arms around little Kristene, hold her and tell her she is safe, loved, protected. She is not damaged or less than.

It is up to me, mentally, to move past the pain and to grow. I know I have the power, the strength, and the desire to heal from this. I am a different person now and I'm starting to feel okay inside—congruent as B says. Lucky. Blessed. Fortunate. I am all of these. I went through a war at home but I survived. B said I will always have tears, sadness and grief over what happened but these will lessen with time and I will have more good days than bad.

June 7 3 p.m.

At session today discussed telling mom about what happened to me—the remembering, the meltdown. Write a letter to her—what I would say to her face to face. I will think about telling her with Alan beside me. There is no way I would do it without him. Good idea for me? As B reminded me the truth will set you free. Need to consider this carefully. Is this the next step in my healing? Alan thinks so. I am not so sure. Want to crawl into myself and camp out there for a while.

Remember this is about me—what is best for me. What I've read about disclosing to family is very few people when they have told their mothers get the reaction, satisfaction, response and so on that they want. What is my reason for wanting/needing ? to tell mom? I know the answer to that one: It is so she will stop the reminiscing (either good or bad) about dad or mentioning his name AT ALL. I am uncertain about the reaction I will get from mom she can be unpredictable. Will she believe me? I am prepared for her not to. Drained. Numb. Tired. Thinking about telling mom is a whole new level of anxiety and what if's.

June 12 9:36 p.m.

Went to a family birthday party today. It was great to see everyone but I was nervous about going. Worried someone would bring up dad. I told myself if there are family pictures, I won't look at them. Worried mom would bring him up. When she mentions him I want to explode and then I am sad afterwards. I am ready to tell her now. God please guide me in this process. It will be difficult and I need to work through my fears—push through them and do it. I am conditioned because of my family dynamics to worry about what others will feel, how they will react, instead of thinking of myself first and what I need. I worry about her reaction—how it will go. Will she believe me? Think about the worst case scenario. Thinking error: imagining the worst. Fear. I have nothing to fear anymore. Be brave. Be unafraid. Own your power and tell her your story.

June 14 8:12 p.m.

I had a disassociation episode at dinner tonight. We were talking about the party and Sam was asking questions about my cousins, my uncles—dad's brothers—and their children. Going through the who's who. I was looking for pictures I had taken at the party and grew extremely agitated while Alan and Sam were talking and I began thinking of my aunt and uncle's house, seeing it as I remembered it as a child and suddenly, poof, my surroundings disappeared. Everything went black. I couldn't hear the guys talking or see anything but darkness. When I came back, seconds, a minute or more? later, they were still talking and my heart was pounding. It scared me that I could do that—be in the same place but also separate from it deep inside myself in some dark void. I know from therapy that this is what I did, where I "went" when I was being hurt by my dad. Another piece of the puzzle falls into place.

I continue to work on soothing my inner child and staying present, staying in the moment, and I know I'm better at this now. Positive inner dialogue for today: You deserve every good thing you've ever had and will have in your life. You are a good person. By telling mom, I am being proactive and taking care of myself by telling the truth. If this had happened to one of my children, I would want to know. That is what guides me.

June 15 10 p.m.

Told mom. Went better than I anticipated. When I started reading the letter I had written and re-written and came to the part where I told her about the meltdown when I remembered what dad had done she stood up, kissed my head and said "He did it to your sister, too." She said Leah had told her a long time ago, after the divorce, but it was when she was using (*drugs*) and saying 'a lot of things' and Mom didn't want to believe her but deep down she knew it was true. She was in denial. (*In September Leah had told me about disclosing the abuse to our mom all those years ago after I told Leah about remembering that our father had sexually abused me, too. Leah said mom wouldn't "hear her" and instead told her how rough her own childhood had been. Leah and I were texting back and forth during this time and checking in on each other. She told me that she had been living with memories of the abuse for years and that our father had sexually abused her throughout her childhood.*

She had never talked to anyone about it. I was angry at our mom for not believing Leah as well as not coming to me to ask if he had abused me as well. Did she know? Not know? Would it have triggered my memories then if my mom had come to me and told me about Leah? I wondered and seethed. I told B that if one of my children had told me they were molested by their father I would immediately ask my other child. Common sense. However, I have learned extremely dysfunctional families like my family of origin operate with a very complex, sick set of rules. Healthy choices and actions are not part of the package.)

Then she fell apart, cried, and said she had no idea he had done it to me. Last fall I didn't know if she knew what had been done to me but of course I wanted to know. She was always working to support us and dad was the primary caregiver. He had access and he was not the man everyone thought he was, obviously, including her. She asked if I was okay and I said yes and then she said she wants me to stay okay and I told her I will. I explained what had happened last fall and I'm in therapy and will be for quite some time. She responded in a loving, maternal way and I needed that. I feel a great relief and unburdening now that she knows.

I told her we never have to speak of it again and she said she doesn't want to talk about it and I am fine with that. She surprised me by asking about the memory, the flashback of molestation when I was 4 or 5, and I described it. She cried out, "You were just a baby!" I told her I was worried she wouldn't believe me and she said of course she believed me who would make that up. Agreed. More relief. My biggest fear from the beginning was not being believed by those who know and love me. I've learned this is a common fear of survivors who disclose. The family and friends who know believe me. Thank God. She may decide to ask me more things later or she may not. Either way I'm good. I AM GOOD. Kristene enhanced.

While I knew Mom had an abusive alcoholic father who she hated, she shared more about what he had done to her. She woke up one night to find him leaning down with his hands moving toward her neck as if to choke her. I encouraged her to seek help, to talk to a therapist because she has so much she has never dealt with. It's no wonder she ended up with my dad. Alcoholism. Abuse. Transgenerational. She cried that she didn't want dad to win. I told her he hasn't. He was sick and he's dead. Mom veering off into her own traumatic past didn't surprise me. I listened some and then we left. I feel less angry at Mom now and at peace. B said 80 to 90 percent of this is mental so I'm working on thinking errors and putting Kristene first. Tonight was a huge step for me in this process. Love yourself Kristene. You have nothing to feel ashamed or guilty about. You did nothing wrong. Life is good. You are good.

June 21 9:48 a.m.

Have had a stretch of good days—not feeling like I could burst into tears or that I have to be on guard. Still anxious in social settings but know now I have always been, have always lived with anxiety, so it is normal for me. Whatever normal is. I'm trying to stay cognizant of any time I begin to feel bad about myself or feel "less than." Not feeling like the little girl in me needs to cry and cry and if she does well that's okay. And of course taking my anxiety medication keeps the inner me from feeling like a volcano about to blow.

Read a helpful book about a woman's experience with PTSD. Her mother had mental problems and her father sexually abused her. I have come a long way from not wanting to think about or read about other people's similar experiences. It helps me feel less alone.

Alan was spot on—telling my mom helped me over another hurdle or was another stepping stone in this process. It has furthered me along.

I've accepted that crying is part of my day now. I was so lost and scared. I resisted and resented for so long having to go through this process. It's made me a better person and I wanted for so long to have my "old" life back. There is no going back only forward with my life and this knowledge. Why would I want my old life back?

Elizabeth's migraines have lessened but now she's having pain in her right side. I called her late last night and she was thinking about going to the ER. I told her if it was that bad to go but she was hesitant. I offered to drive up there and go with her but she said she wanted to wait and call the doctor in the morning. I hate that she's an hour away and feeling sick and in pain.

6/23 2:42 p.m

At my session today, we talked about disclosing to mom and her reaction. B affirmed it was helpful mom reacted in a comforting, loving way, and she believed me. B said it helped the little Kristene inside grow up some because she was able to tell her mom what was done to her. I have always felt loved by mom. The initial, intense anger I felt for her choices and actions as I was growing up has left me. I have forgiven her for not being there for us.

A flash: dad dragging Leah to her bedroom, slamming her door, hearing him beating her, her cries and screams while mom and I sat at the dinner table. I stare down at my plate of food and sob. Mom saying, 'Shut up and eat your dinner.' I was maybe 7? 8? 9? Anger, sadness, fear and confusion because she didn't stop dad from abusing her. I understand it now because she was repeating a pattern of her childhood but I am allowed to feel angry and sad about it. My parents' marriage was a messy one and ended as a war fueled with infidelity, anger, resentment, alcohol, and abuse. Mom enabled dad's behavior for 16 years. Shame on her. Shame on him. My sister and I were the casualties of that war. In the end, what happened between my parents is their story. Leah and I were simply fighting to survive.

Releasing my anger and sadness eases the depression. When I'm angry I need to release it in healthy ways. Write it out. Walk it out. Talk it out. Anything but hold it in any longer.

June 25 3:20 p.m.
I've been thinking about forgiveness. Forgiving dad. Does forgiving mean saying what someone did to hurt you is okay?. No. It's about freeing yourself. Freeing yourself from the person who hurt you. I hate him for what he did. He stole our innocence. Our childhoods. Can I forgive him because he

was sick? Sometimes I try to get there, test it out, say the words but I don't feel deep down yet that I can forgive him. I am free of what happened to me in the past or am I? I'd like to ask him why he did it. If he were alive, you betcha I would confront him about it, but I can't. And I've learned to be okay with that. I've written my letters to him and ripped them up. I don't want revenge. He knows what he did. He must have really hated himself to hurt his own children. The point of my healing and moving forward is not about his sickness. It's about what I need. My voice and giving a voice to the little girl who had none.

I cried in the pool, the deep, deep, wailing cry which brought relief, left me drained.

June 26 2:41 p.m.

I mowed the lawn—it is 90 degrees—and it felt invigorating to move and sweat. A release. Pull weeds, trim bushes. Physical activity has helped my PTSD symptoms. I am practicing being patient with myself when I am nervous over simple things or when my paranoia kicks in. One change yesterday, I didn't need to take anxiety medicine before we went to a party. My social anxiety is still there but has improved. I'll take it.

Elizabeth is having a Cat Scan and insisted I didn't need to go with her. Praying something is found to explain the pain but of course not something serious.

JULY

July 3 2:35 p.m.

Elizabeth's Cat Scan came back and it showed spots on her liver. She has MRI on Wed. Trying not to panic. I told Elizabeth I wouldn't Google it but Sam did and then I did. One site said it can be cysts which are harmless and another site listed more grim possibilities. I'm praying they are cysts. The site said estrogen production can cause them. Her pain is on her right side and lower abdomen. Whatever happens I know God she is in Your hands. Help us all through this anxious time.

I've been busy getting ready for our 4th of July party which I couldn't care about now that this is going on with Elizabeth.

A new tactic for letting out my anger towards dad is imagining him when I'm mowing, he's all the slender blades of grass chopped to bits. Or scrubbing something clean—he's the dirt I'm washing away. Remember anger is pain. When I hold onto the anger it only hurts me. B said at some point I won't even need my anxiety medication. She said I will always be angry at dad and sad for what happened. I understand this and accept it. But it will not keep me from enjoying life and all of the love, laughter, happiness and goodness I deserve.

July 15

So much has happened over the past two weeks. Had an appt for a check up with Dr. G and we talked about the meltdown as we always do and it felt therapeutic this time. Felt invigorated afterwards. She said I've been given the gift of enlightenment and some people die never knowing, never remembering, that this same thing happened to them and have lived with struggles and problems their entire lives never knowing the root cause. It reminded me to be grateful for the knowledge I have. I have been on Lamictal as a mood stablilizer for years but I am going to begin weaning off of it. I don't need it—I know the root of my issues and I don't want to take a medication I no longer need.

The spots on Elizabeth's liver are benign. Thank God. But she is still not feeling well. I think it's her gallbladder and she spent the night in the hospital but the HIDA scan showed no issue with it so the surgeon wants to wait. I went through same thing when I was 40—every test showed my gallbladder was normal but it wasn't. I wanted to yell at the surgeon to just take it out. I've hit the wall. Trying not to get overwhelmed with Elizabeth's health issues but she has had too many and I'm a mom and moms worry. I am so much better now and when the anxiety builds I cry and feel the sadness, the release, let it out and out and out.

I told Alan yesterday if someone came up to me and said, "I heard you had a psychotic break when you remembered you were molested by your dad." I would unashamedly say, "Yes. You are right. That happened." Three short, simple, sentences which speak volumes about how far I've come in this process.

July 18 1:04 p.m.

Thinking back about how frustrated and angry I was at myself, at my mind, in the beginning as if my mind betrayed me. Opened Pandora's box. Secrets, anger, sadness, pain. All I'd held inside released. Dr. G asked if I'd forgiven my parents for the neglect and I said yes to mom and no to dad. She said forgiveness is about not allowing the person who hurt you to have power over you. For me forgiveness has always been part of the equation but am I really ready to forgive or just give lip service to it? I will always be sad and angry about the abuse whether I forgive him or not. Do I have to forgive to fully heal? I want to forgive because that is part of moving on. I am healing but healing goes on whether or not I forgive him. For me, it's not the end point but another step along the way.

July 21 4:34 p.m.

Saw surgeon yesterday. Elizabeth has gallbladder out next Thurs. RELIEVED finally something is being done. The surgeon said she will look at her appendix and the spots on her liver while she is in there and I'm happy about that. Even though she hasn't felt the best this summer her headaches are better and she's had a much better summer than last year. Hate when my children don't feel well and wish it were me instead. My prayer today is she heals quickly, as quickly as Sam did after his surgery.

Saw B on Tuesday—had been 3 ½ weeks. Productive session—good to go as always. So much to process afterwards. Had not been reflecting much on my past and grieving and I need to refocus or I will slip back. I'm feeling much stronger now. Told her I'm handling Elizabeth's health issues better this year than I did last year at this time. B said it's because there is more room in my bucket. I bought a book on reclaiming your inner child. So much to read and do at times. This healing is hard work and it is overwhelming at times. It's a messy process and the control freak in me doesn't like that. I still, from time to time, want a checklist to complete and move on. NOT how it works.

July 26 4:49 p.m.

Going to the fair tonight for dinner—love fair food!

I'm paying attention to the times when I'm overwhelmed and I tell myself it is okay to curl up on the couch with my blanket and watch television or shut out the world to think and reflect. I am more patient now with myself…not as hard on myself as I have always been. The mind is incredibly amazing. How I blocked the painful in order to survive. How I remembered after all this time. It was as if I had placed all of the negative and painful parts of my childhood in boxes and one by one they began tumbling from a high shelf and spilled open. I want freedom from the past. I am feeling like my outside is matching my inside lately. No more "pretending normal." No more front. Since the meltdown and working through a lifetime of issues, I feel like the real me for the first time and THIS feels like freedom.

July 27 5:29 p.m.

My prayer for today is Elizabeth's surgery goes well tomorrow and she has a swift recovery. This kid has had enough health issues God and I'd like to put an order in that she have no more—she's met her quota please! Thinking of her having another surgery brings up memories of her back surgeries and the excruciating pain she was in. How helpless and overwhelmed I felt. How I wanted it to be me instead of her. Today my bucket was filling up again so I cried and cried.

July 29 11:38 a.m.

Surgery was a success. Surgeon said gallbladder had been inflamed previously. She took a large nodule off her liver and it will be biopsied along with gallbladder. Elizabeth is asleep on the couch. The pain meds knocked her out and I hope she sleeps all day. I brought plenty of books and Sam's laptop to keep my mind occupied. I was emotional seeing Elizabeth on the gurney before they took her to the operating room. I kissed her on the forehead and told her I loved her. My mind flashed to 12 years ago and it was her once more at 14 going in for her first back surgery. Scared but brave.

How I stuffed all of my emotions for so long, as B said, it's a wonder I don't have a physical illness from it. I never realized how much anger, resentment and pain I had inside. While this past year has completely sucked going through this,

I am grateful I know why I stuff my emotions. Now my job is to work at not doing it any longer.

I am thankful I can be here with Elizabeth to help her after surgery. Thank you God that I have the time to think, reflect, heal and deal with my past.

Alan said he had a dream where I told him I can do whatever I want to do because of what I went through and I kept repeating this to him and he kept saying I know. I don't know what that dream means but I told him that I don't want him to baby me because of my past—I never want anyone's pity, including his. All I need is his love and support and he's given me both.

I was handed shame as a child, handed a sick secret to keep, and now I can release it. I read an article on a site for survivors of sexual assault and the author was talking about the phrase "get over it" and how when this is said to sexual abuse victims it is not only cruel but inaccurate. In the beginning, I thought that was my goal. One day I would be over it. Well I was wrong that is for sure. You make it through and at some point you move on but the healing continues. I had to accept there is no "end" when you have been molested as a child. The article gave me clarity on this issue and validated my feelings. The article said that phrase can make people internalize their shame as if they are not strong enough to "get over it." Well, sit right down here people and let me tell you about "getting over" remembering you were molested as a young child by a parent. It's a terrible phrase. I will always live with the effects of the abuse. I am learning how to live with them in a healthy way.

AUGUST

Aug. 1 1:27 p.m.

Home from Elizabeth's—feel strongly she's on the mend. She's still feeling nauseous but is able to keep bland food down and stay by herself. My anxiety has been through the roof and I couldn't sleep well at her house. I see B tomorrow so I am back to thinking about this journey I'm on. Forgiveness. I can forgive because it is what I have to do for myself. If I don't, it only holds me back and I have to move forward.

8/2 5:30 p.m.

B said I was spared by not remembering until last summer. At first when she said this it angered me. Spared?! I was molested I wasn't spared! But when I thought about it, even though it doesn't take the pain away, it is another vantage point for me to view my past. My life could have turned out so differently if I had remembered all along as Leah had. I could have turned to drugs and alcohol to numb myself. I could have had a string of bad relationships or married an alcoholic or drug addict or become one. So in that sense, I was spared. My mind protected me.

8/3/16 11:12 a.m.

Had a flashback yesterday. I picked up a pair of my flip-flops off the floor and saw a violent moment from my past. Things I had forgotten or stored away a long time ago resurface now and again and it can be alarming like a lightning strike and I go numb. PTSD sucks but I no longer have the intense fears and dread I had this past winter. Celebrate yourself woman! You are strong. You are a miracle. As B said I take care of everyone else now it's time to take care of myself.

8/4/16

B said one day I will file away this experience as something terrible that happened and I will move on. She said not to worry or try to think about what grieving stage I'm in because the "where" I am in this process does not matter. I still want that damn checklist, or hurdle to jump, so I can move on. Just let go and feel—feel it all. Think about it and continue to stay healthy.

8/7/16 9:01 a.m.

Alan and I went away for our 28th anniversary. Had a good time—much needed break for both of us. Took a paddle boat ride, went to a baseball game, and slept and ate. Perfect weekend. Anxious about heading home today but it's the re-entry—back to the real world. The phrase 'wherever you go, there you are' popped into my head again as it has many times this past year. I can't escape reality even though at times the old me would like to run from it. Forgiveness is a choice I have decided I can make. If I don't forgive, it does too much damage to me, takes away my serenity. While I know poof! the pain won't be gone, I do know not forgiving is an obstacle to my freedom and happiness.

8/10/16

I've come far and I'm eternally grateful for that—I never thought I would say I am grateful I had the meltdown but I am. I may never have more pieces to the puzzle of my childhood, more flashbacks, but I know enough. I know and that is enough. I will always be emotional about it but not so deeply—it won't hurt as sharply as time goes by. It will go in the file folder of my life one of these days. I've accepted I will always have trust issues, always hold parts of myself back but this does not make me defective. I needed to face that I have always, deep down, been ashamed of my family—the divorce, abandonment, alcoholism, physical and verbal abuse. I had tackled these issues in Al-Anon years ago and then wham this new piece of my past surfaced last September. A huge piece of the puzzle that made so much of my early childhood make sense. This has been the biggest struggle of my life but I'm making it. Last night Alan gave me a huge bear hug and asked how I was doing and I laughed and said, 'Well I no longer want to off myself.' My sick humor. But he gets it. He's been with me throughout this whole journey and he is my rock but I also know I am my own rock. When he held me one night long ago and I said I don't think I can do this anymore he said 'Yes you can. You are strong. You are Wonder Woman.' I disagreed with him then but today I would agree. Survivors are Wonder Women and Men. Alan was strong for me when I couldn't be for myself and that is what 28 years of marriage looks like for us. True love. For the first time, I know I deserve every good thing I have, as B tells me over and over. I am no longer afraid of this truth or of my feelings.

8/11 4:27 p.m

Yesterday afternoon I wrote my final letter to my dad. It was pure anguish but I told him why I was forgiving him— for myself. I told him I hate what he did to me but I don't hate him any longer. I severed the connection. He is nothing to me. I'm at peace with my decision to forgive him. I unbound myself from the tie that was binding me. Strangling me.

8/14/16 5:30 p.m.

Yesterday when I was in the bathroom upstairs getting ready for a wedding I was putting on make-up and stepped back from the mirror and thought, "Holy cow, sister, look at all that has happened to you in such a short amount of time." August. One year ago. Leading up to the meltdown. Another marker of time… "anniversary of". B reminds me of this in therapy when I am too hard on myself and yesterday for the first time, click, I got it. It sunk in or I came to a full awareness of it. I am able to finally see it.

Feelings. What am I feeling now? While I'd like, at times, to burn down the three houses I lived in with my parents and sister, and smash my dad's headstone to pieces or better yet dig up his bones and stomp on them I can't, but visualizing this is enough to release the anger...open the valve and let out some steam. It's satisfying. I can feel anything and everything now that I need, have, to feel and THAT feels amazing. I am not stuck and silent and suffering. I have my voice.

8/15

Had lunch with Alan, Sam and the Hamilton's (*family friends*). Did not feel like spending the entire afternoon alone. Go through these moments when I have to be around other people to feel less isolated. Other times solitude for the entire day is what I need. Feeling again like I need to see an end to this—to these feelings the sadness that envelops me. B says there will be an end. I trust her and believe her. Feeling more emotional than I have been lately and feeling alone in this even though I know I'm not alone—I have my supports in place. I haven't talked to Alan about it in a while. I know he just wants to know I'm okay. I wish I could press a fast forward button and be a 'thriver.'

Feel positive about my decision I can forgive dad. I can't hang on to the depth of anger and the intensity of hate for him that I felt early on. What he did is unforgiveable and as I work and process through the layers of anger and really think deeply about it the only way for me to be free and live fully is to forgive for myself and my sanity. It has been an emotional choice to come to terms with but it is the right one at the right time. More tears. More release. Remember Kristene—no timetable. That's a thinking error. Positive positive positive. I have less of an urge to fill my days with anything to stay busy so I don't have to feel to avoid. Working at finding a balance of reflecting on what happened and living in the moment. It is HARD. Feel vulnerable—and it's a strange feeling for me. I begin my 100 mg of Lamictal tonight. I pray I am able to handle the decrease. I am fine—I have dug my way out of the avalanche and you are HERE—the worst is over. The hardest part of the journey is behind you. Celebrate your awesomeness!

Aug. 19 10:47 a.m.

Work on yourself—it's not selfish it's what you need Kristene. It's a breezy morning and I'm on the porch listening to the birds chitter in chorus. Wonderful to have a languid, lazy morning. Alan and I went to the state fair again last night— loved holding hands walking around and eating. Faith instead of fear. God has me in the palms of his hands.

8/22/16 10:05 a.m.

Feeling lethargic since dropping to 100 mg of Lamictal and some slight headaches but not feeling as teary anymore. Confident and feeling that I am going to be okay—I'm not going to forever stay stuck in a cycle of self-hatred, shame, regret and grieving. Am I minimizing again? No I think I'm further along with acceptance. I see B tomorrow at 11 and I'm glad—it's a physical need almost now my body/mind knows when I need to talk with her. She steers me toward healthy thinking. Honesty. Truth. Living fully.

8/23

Discussed with B my need to forgive dad. She asked why and I told her for myself to move on. She said some people don't need to forgive in order to move forward but because of the type of person I am I do. It's part of the acceptance process. I came to the realization at the end of the session that I don't love dad. I thought I still did or that I had to because he was my father. What I feel instead is nostalgia for the family rituals—the good times—I can recall when the four of us were a family. Holidays and Friday night pizza. Long stretches of time from my childhood are missing and I know it's because I lived in my own protective bubble. B said the opposite of love is neutrality not hate. I hate what he did but I don't hate him anymore. I feel nothing for him. B said I may go back and forth forgiving and that's normal. I've been thinking about forgiveness for a long time so I know I truly have. I've always felt protective of my family and I was conditioned to hide the truth and put on a front. A memory: I shared with a friend that mom was angry and threw a fit because I asked dad to walk me down the aisle at my wedding. We had a huge fight and she stopped speaking to me. My friend went on her own to talk to mom about it because I was upset and mom told me later I should not have told anyone about her behavior—betrayal on my part. Me, the smoother-over, the people pleaser, apologized and sent flowers to mom. It wasn't until later I realized mom should have never asked that of me. It was my wedding. Unfair and immature. Self-serving. Temperamental. Now had I known then what he had done then hell no he would not have been at my wedding.

I told Alan on the ride over to therapy and then told B during my session I feel, for the first time in a long time, maybe my entire life, REAL.

B said I'm the sole survivor in my family—I'm not an alcoholic or drug abuser or had a string of failed relationships. She said I'm a wonderful mother and wife. I cried when she was saying these things. I know it's true and I struggled so hard and so long to be the opposite of my family. Thank God for this. Thank God for little Kristene whose mind protected her.

Aug. 24 2:42 p.m.

Spent time in the pool yesterday and had time to reflect. The water calms me and I float and think best when I am in there. It also soothes the little girl in me because I am doing something I spent hours doing as a young girl—riding my bike to the park pool and staying all day. Yesterday's session left me drained and feeling effects of going off my medication. We discussed setbacks yesterday and B asked if I knew what those would look like. I imagined the extreme—doubting the abuse occurred (which I wouldn't because I know it did) or being so depressed I would be unable to get of bed (possible but I know the depression I have now is mild and I am handling it okay). She said it could be those but also panic attacks or struggling at work. I have not had a panic attack for several weeks—anxiety yes but controllable. As B said everyone has some form of anxiety in certain situations.

Setbacks—why it is important I see her every two weeks. I am making such good progress and the depression and anger do not scare me anymore. Neither does having PTSD as it did in the beginning when I was overwhelmed and exhausted. What was happening to me—AHHHHHH! Trust yourself and the road you are on—progress and healing.

I am grateful today for God's love and guidance. My prayer is one of thanks for giving me this life, my family, and my faith. Help me to open myself to trust each day for your plan for my life. To let go of fear and trust completely.

Aug. 31 3:39 p.m.

Decided it was time to drive to the three homes I lived in with my parents and Leah and then go to the cemetery to look at dad's headstone.

Something mom said when I disclosed to her triggered the notion to do this—had thought about doing it a long time ago but couldn't. After I told her about the flashback of abuse on Northwest St. she told me she can't even look at the house when she drives by the street. I told her I can't either. Then I began thinking I'm not going to let the abuse by dad keep me from looking or even glancing at a house we lived in. That gives the abuse power over me. I only remember my first home through pictures and mom's stories of living there because we moved to the Northwest Street home soon after. This house is the first one I remember. I stopped in front of it and looked it over—seeing it in my mind as I remember it as a young girl. The tall tree by the front steps is gone. Also the porch swing. As I stared at the house and the memories appeared, my arms and legs went weak and I felt a tingling sensation in my crotch as if I was being touched. It felt like I was going to wet my pants—a flashback of how I felt when dad was abusing me. A visceral, physical response. Pictures of the interior and back yard flashed in my mind. Next drove out to Jones Road house. I did not park in front of the house just drove slowly by. More pictures in my head.

At cemetery I stared at his headstone. Did not feel intense anger or hatred in fact I felt nothing—absent of all feelings/emotions while I was there. Told him he's no longer worth my time or energy and that I stopped loving him or the idea I had of him long, long ago. It felt freeing. I thought I'd never want to look at those three houses again but felt like I had to face the places where the abuse happened. If I could, I would go inside each one walk around and look at the rooms and hope in doing so it would trigger more memories but I can't and that's okay. I don't need to in order to move forward. I am my father's daughter but he never deserved me. I read in one of my books about healing that a parent who sexually abuses their children is just a child molester who stays at home. That was my dad. Even before I remembered sexual abuse, if someone were to ask me if I loved my dad I would have answered, "No, but when I was a child I did." I realize inside me exists a little girl who used to love her dad, who has a few good memories of him, and that will never change. It's a small part, but it's there and it can never be cut out and disposed of, forgotten. I'm okay with keeping those few memories and the nostalgia they bring with them.

September

9/1/16 1:30 p.m.

Circled on the calendar my 1 year marks—9/8/15 visit to the stress center—the day my world crashed around me. 9/9/15 Alan took me to Dr. G. and I remembered. 9/15/15 first visit to B. Milestones. Those six days between are lost to me. I have no memories of what I did or said or where I went.

I made it through the first year. My life changed forever that September. Shifted. Altered permanently. A time for reflection this month. So happy I made it. Relieved—I survived. I will keep going, growing and healing. I'm exhausted physically and mentally but I am FREE.

9/2/16 9:50 a.m.

Dreamed I was walking down a road with many other people I did not know and a man stopped us and said we had to take a detour. He pointed toward a building and a group of strange, creepy men directed us down dark, narrow steps. I knew they were lying and evil but they forced us to go down with them. No one in the group spoke. We just did as we were told. It was dark and gray and many people were trapped in cages. I stood at the bottom of the steps looking up at the doorway and the bright light outside it and thought this is not going to happen to me—I will not be held captive by them. I charged up the steps and ran and ran.

What a metaphor for my experience as a child and this past year—one for my entire life. Keep going. I am a different person now—this experience changed my life; how could it not? I am less judgmental, less angry. I put the focus on me and how I can improve myself. I give myself so much more credit now for surviving and accomplishing all that I have. I am honest with myself and others and I take better care of myself. I TRUST I am exactly where I need to be learning what I need to learn and growing.

Sept. 6 7:10 p.m.

Today B said I corrected a thinking error by visiting my childhood homes instead of avoiding them and we discussed the flashback. She told me it took an incredible mind (mine!) to overcome the abuse and make the choices I did—school, friends, college, marriage to a healthy man. She said, 'Kristene you have no idea what a miracle that is.' Which made me cry. I never saw it that way—I just knew what I didn't want. I wanted the opposite of my circumstances and I strove to make better choices than my parents and Leah. B asked if I felt a sense of peace when I was standing at my dad's grave and I said no but it felt cleansing. She said that's a good word for it. I don't know if I will ever feel a sense of peace with what dad did. How can

I feel peace for my dad when I know what he did and who he really was?

9/8/16

Well it's the 1 year anniversary of my meltdown. On this day last year Alan had his stress test. I hazily recall sitting in a chair across the room from him watching as he lay on a bed in a hospital gown. I was there but I wasn't. That day, Alan would tell me later, is when he drove me to the stress center. Alan told me he noticed a change in me when I quit teaching. Had the psychosis started then? Slowly building? I told B at one session when I think back to that time leading up to the meltdown I felt as if I were being pushed along a trajectory not of my own volition; captive to wherever it took me. Teary thinking of last September but that is the past. Proud of how far I've come in a year. No more pretend normal. What a difference a year makes. Thank you God for my life, for every experience, both positive and negative, has made me the person I am today. I am strong, wise and loving and I trust my healing process and the path I am on at last. Gratitude. Peace. Love. Hope. Trust. I AM REAL.

EPILOGUE

We aren't the weeds in the cracks of life. We're the strong, amazing flowers that found a way to grow in the most challenging conditions.

Jeane McElvaney

I continue to journal and heal. I learned to accept that the abuse is part of my story. It saddens me that this is so but I have made peace with this knowledge. One theme in my journal is repetition of thoughts as I moved back and forth between the grief stages. I bemoaned to my therapist at one session that I considered stopping my journal because it felt like I was writing the same things over and over. She said "That means you need to say them." I know now I had to say them, and perhaps will in the future, to remind myself, encourage myself, and soothe myself when I am overwhelmed. I was learning to live with a long-buried, terrible piece of my past.

On deciding to forgive my father: I chose to forgive him because he was an extremely sick and damaged human being.

I struggled with forgiving him because it was not something I wanted to do—how does one forgive something so terrible? However, I knew in order to have peace and move forward in my life, forgiveness was the answer. In a single day, I would practice forgiveness for him and then moments later I was back to unforgiving him. I read an article once about a man who forgave his wife's killer. He said that forgiveness is an act, separate from emotion, and that he simply decided to forgive. I disagree. Emotion and forgiveness are inextricably bound. One cannot forgive unless one lets go of the emotional ties that bind. One has to decide on his or her own terms and timetable when to unbind themselves. Was it necessary for me to forgive in order to heal? For me, yes. It was part of accepting what my father had done to me. For other survivors, no. Everyone's journey to heal is different. I only know with much time and thought and compassion for myself, in forgiving I reclaimed the power my father stole from me as a child.

My father hurt my sister and me in the deepest ways a parent can hurt a child—in body, mind and spirit. It saddens and angers me to know Leah and I suffered at his hands and it affected our lives in profound ways. After my parents divorced, I carried a silent shame of him my entire life for choices he made—the emotional, verbal and physical abuse I remembered, the affair, his lies, the abandonment and refusal to pay child support. But that shame was his to carry and never mine.

I have come to realize I had three childhoods. Childhood number one holds the events I had remembered through age 11 when my parents were married. Memories from this time are like snapshots; events encapsulated and isolated in my mind. Childhood number two carries a rich store of memories after my father left. Remembrances from this time are fluid and flow through my mind in a clear narrative. Childhood number three appeared with the psychotic break and contains the most vital truth about my childhood—the sexual abuse by my father. This childhood is a vault my mind opened and allowed me to peer into and see the truth.

What I learned on my healing journey is that every Survivor's story is as unique as his or her fingerprints. In my case, I remembered I was molested by my father and then flashbacks of the abuse appeared throughout the months following the psychotic break. In short, I knew he sexually abused me—I had the knowledge first—and then my mind allowed me to see, feel, and smell details. In the future, my mind may show me more pictures, the vault may open, and if it does I know they are pieces of the puzzle to my past and they appear because I need to know them. They are gifts. I do not fear them.

If I had not remembered the molestation, not had the psychotic break, then I would have continued suffering from depression, anxiety, intense feelings of anger, and the oppressing need to control without knowing the root cause. And my family would have suffered as well.

I remembered. I know the truth. I feel joy at the beauty of these two simple, profound statements because I am free for the first time in my life. My story is my badge of courage. What my body had been feeling all of those years, the depression on and off since I was a teenager, the suicidal thinking, the anxiety, and the fears make sense now. I can finally feel my feelings and work at handling people, places and situations which trigger my PTSD. With therapy, journaling, and the emotional support and patience from Alan I am healing at last. I'm lucky, fortunate, grateful and supremely blessed (and any other positive adjective in any language known to humankind) to have my husband, two adult children, and friends who care and love me.

Beauty exists in knowing the truth no matter how awful the truth may be. Freedom comes in facing that truth and moving on. I was given the gift of knowing the truth. I was handed that gift of power by my mind and my body and I thank God for that.

In September of 2015, I remembered. What did I do with what was done to me as a child? I grieved. I accepted. I forgave. I am free, whole, and healthy.

A Note to Survivors

Whether you always remembered the abuse but never told, suspect you were abused, or, like me, remembered years later, it is never too late to receive help. You are not alone. I urge you to tell someone you trust and then find a therapist or healing group. You deserve to heal no matter how much time has passed since the abuse. Do not suffer in silence because silence kills souls and relationships and dreams and cuts short lives. I was at the point several times early on when the thought of swallowing a bottle of pills made more sense, offered more hope, more relief, an escape from my suffering. But I decided I wanted to live and could live with what happened. I deserved a happy, healthy, whole life and to achieve this the only path was facing the truth, doing the grueling work of recovery, and walking through the fire. As Beverly Engel, author of *The Right to Innocence: Healing the Trauma of Childhood Sexual Abuse*, wrote "If you were sexually abused as a child, you are still suffering from its impact as an adult. Childhood sexual abuse is such an overwhelming, damaging, and humiliating assault on a child's mind, soul and body that he or she cannot escape emotional damage. The abuse invades every facet of one's sexuality, one's ability to be successful, one's ability to trust others, and physical health. It causes its victims to be self-destructive, overcontrolling, and abusive to others, as well as addiction to alcohol, drugs and food and attraction to love partners who abuse them physically, verbally, and emotionally. Its victims come to feel ashamed, guilty, powerless, depressed, afraid and angry. Whether you actually remember the abuse or not, the damage caused by the abuse only increases with time."

Bibliography for Survivors

The Courage to Heal: A Guide for Women Survivors of Child Sexual Abuse by Ellen Bass and Laura Davis

The Right to Innocence: Healing the Trauma of Childhood Sexual Abuse by Beverly Engel, M.F. C.C.

The Body Keeps the Score: Brain, Mind, and Body in the Healing of Trauma by Bessel Van Der Kolk, M.D.

No Comfort Zone: Notes on Living with Post Traumatic Stress Disorder by Marla Handy

Betrayal of Innocence: Incest and its Devastation by Dr. Susan Forward and Craig Buck

Forgiving Our Parents Forgiving Ourselves by Dr. David Stoop

Forgiving the Unforgiveable: Overcoming the Bitter Legacy of Intimate Wounds by Beverly Flanigan, M.S.S.W.

Hush by Nicole Braddock Bromley

Healing Insights: Effects of Abuse for Adults Abused as Children by Jeanne McElvaney

www.ingramcontent.com/pod-product-compliance
Lightning Source LLC
Chambersburg PA
CBHW022335280326
41934CB00006B/640